David
This is where it all reall[illegible]
us when 'Keppel' becam[illegible]
Happy readin[illegible]

Dec. 2002.

SHIP WITHOUT WATER

The Story of HMS Daedalus II

by

GRAHAM BEBBINGTON

with a foreword by
Rear Admiral Iain Henderson CBE RN
Flag Officer Naval Aviation

CHURNET VALLEY BOOKS
43 Bath Street, Leek, Staffordshire. 01538 399033
email: picture.book@virgin.net web: freespace.virgin.net/c.hinton/

ISBN 1 897949 63 4

Dedicated to all those men and women who served with HMS Daedalus at Newcastle-under-Lyme.

Acknowledgements

I am especially grateful to Rear Admiral Iain Henderson CBE RN, Flag Officer Naval Aviation for writing the foreword, and also to his Secretary, Commander Rob Nairn for his kind assistance during my research.

Special thanks are also due to Malcolm Williams whose love of the village of Clayton and enthusiasm for the story of Daedalus II inspired me to research this work.

In addition to those quoted in the text or source notes, I acknowledge most gratefully the assistance of the following: Mrs M E Graham, Mrs A Walker, Lt. Cdr. E W Whitley RN Ret'd., Mr J A Derry, Robert H Bowers, Richard A Durrant, Peter B Pellington, Derek Silverton, Ray C Sturtivant, Leonard (Tiny) Mitchell, and Councillor Mrs Elizabeth Caddy JP.

I must also record my gratitude to Steve Meys (Deputy Head, Clayton High School); Janet Adamson, Folkestone Library; Alan King, Local & Naval Studies Librarian, Portsmouth Library; Neil Somerville, BBC Archives; Mrs DMA Randall, Head of Archive Services, Staffs County Council; the Librarian and staff of Newcastle-under-Lyme and Clayton Libraries; Mr FR Harley, Chief Executive and staff of Newcastle Borough Council; The Secretary, The Association of Royal Navy Officers; the Editors of Navy News, The Wren and the Sentinel respectively and particularly to John Abberley; and the staff of the Fleet Air Museum, Yeovilton; Royal Naval Museum, Portsmouth; and the Imperial War Museum, in particular Peter Simkins.

I am also deeply indebted to Dr Joan Delin for making extremely valuable suggestions to my final draft. My thanks to Christine at Churnet Valley. Also to John Grindey for additional artwork.

Finally, my wife Lynne Margaret has shared in all the pains and pleasures of research and, as usual, assisted with everything from typing to proof reading.

Foreword

I was delighted to be asked to write this foreword on a unique chapter of Fleet Air Arm history. DAEDALUS is a name known throughout the Royal Navy because of the Air Engineering training establishment at Lee-on-Solent (now sadly closed), whilst DAEDALUS II remained eclipsed by its headquarters establishment bearing the same name.

How good it is, therefore, that Graham Bebbington has now put DAEDALUS II firmly on the map through a huge amount of painstaking research. The result is a most comprehensive piece of work which, besides being a very interesting read, will take its place as a useful historical record of a Fleet Air Arm establishment whose star, though it may have only shone briefly, nevertheless shone brightly.

IAIN HENDERSON CBE RN
Rear Admiral
Flag Officer Naval Aviation

Also by Graham Bebbington

The Loggerheads Project (Newcastle Borough Council)

Pit Boy to Prime Minister (University of Keele)

A Brief Life (Isle of Wight County Press)

Trentham at War (Churnet Valley Books)

2nd Benbow Divisional Guard with Lieut. E. Hendy in charge, taken at the front of a camouflaged Clayton Hall, 1944.
Source Clayton Library

Contents

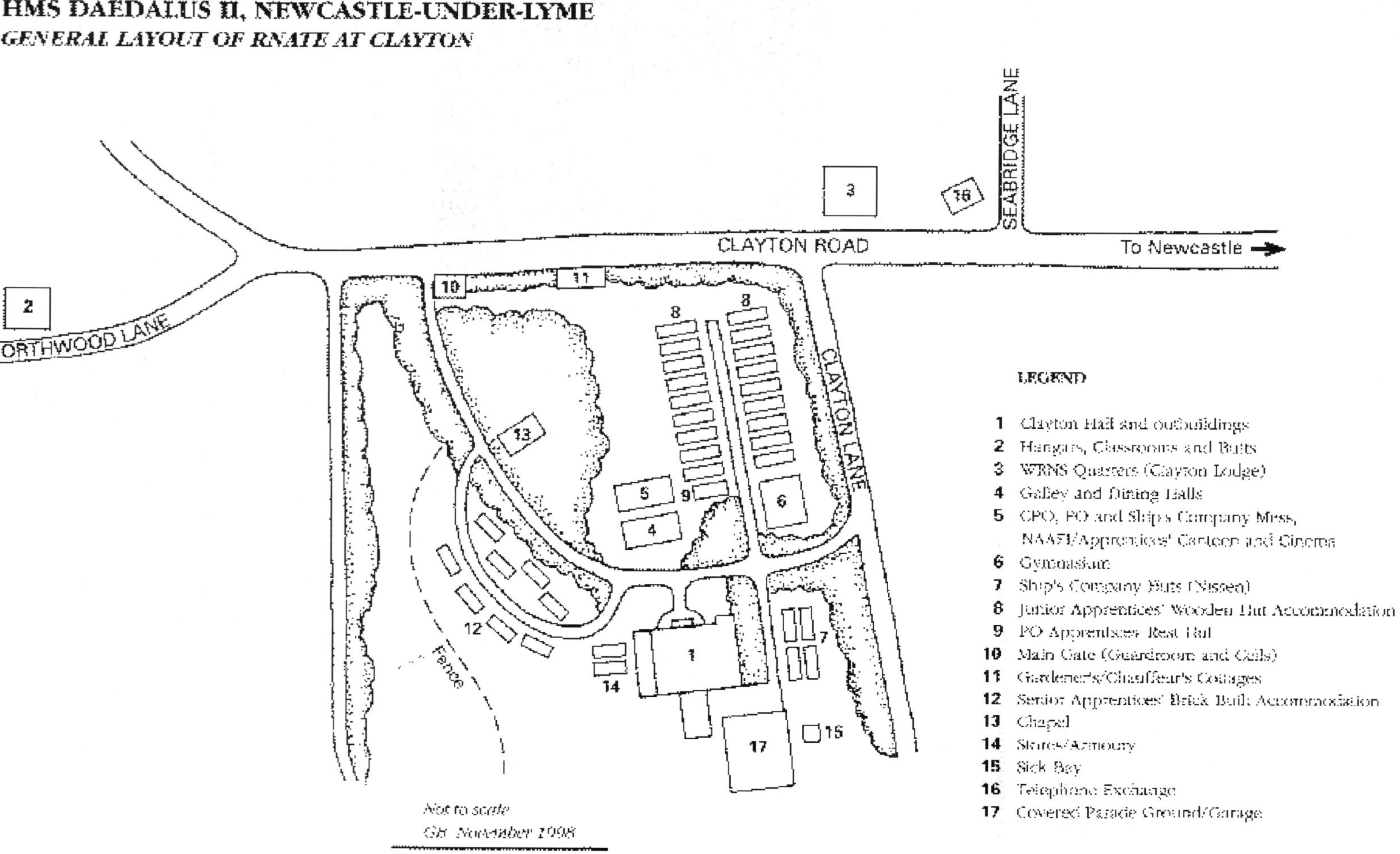
HMS DAEDALUS II, NEWCASTLE-UNDER-LYME
GENERAL LAYOUT OF RNATE AT CLAYTON
NORTHWOOD LANE
CLAYTON ROAD
SEABRIDGE LANE
To Newcastle
CLAYTON LANE
Fence
Not to scale
GR November 1998
LEGEND
1 Clayton Hall and outbuildings
2 Hangars, Classrooms and Butts
3 WRNS Quarters (Clayton Lodge)
4 Galley and Dining Halls
5 CPO, PO and Ship's Company Mess, NAAFI/Apprentices' Canteen and Cinema
6 Gymnasium
7 Ship's Company Huts (Nissen)
8 Junior Apprentices' Wooden Hut Accommodation
9 PO Apprentices' Rest Hut
10 Main Gate (Guardroom and Cells)
11 Gardener's/Chauffeur's Cottages
12 Senior Apprentices' Brick Built Accommodation
13 Chapel
14 Stores/Armoury
15 Sick Bay
16 Telephone Exchange
17 Covered Parade Ground/Garage

Introduction

Although situated in the Heart of England, Staffordshire has a surprisingly strong naval tradition. For example, the County boasts a number of famous seafaring sons including Admiral Lord George Anson (1697-1762), John Jervis, Admiral Lord St.Vincent (1735-1823) and, of course, Captain Edward Smith (1850-1912) of the ill fated Titanic. Moreover, the Borough of Newcastle-under-Lyme, the area principally concerned in this work, lays claim to the birthplace of Sir Joseph Cook (1860-1947) the 'father' of the Australian Navy, and Canon Henry Moseley (1801-1872) who devised the formulae by which the dynamical stability of ships were calculated. It also has strong associations with Admiral Rowland Mainwaring (1783-1862) and Admiral Smith Child (1730-1813).

Even so, there are those who may have difficulty in accepting the fact that there was an HMS Daedalus at Clayton during World War II. Indeed, having attempted to explain this to some, resultant expressions have led me to believe that they are either questioning my sanity, or perhaps trying to imagine what happened to the vast area of water which enabled a ship of the line to sail into a suburb of Newcastle-under-Lyme! The fact is, of course, that HMS Daedalus (also known as Daedalus II) was a land based establishment or, to use naval terms, a 'stone frigate.'

Confused? Apparently, so were the Germans! According to a number of sources, the traitor William Joyce was said to have announced from Germany that 'Daedalus has sunk!'. Joyce, of course, was the notorious 'Lord Haw-Haw' whose propaganda broadcasts were designed to sap the resolve of Britain during the dark years of World War II.

Traitor William Joyce, otherwise known as Lord Haw-Haw, the notorious wartime broadcaster for Nazi Germany who informed his listeners that Daedalus had sunk. After the war he was hanged.
Courtesy Sentinel Newspapers.

Clayton's Daedalus II was a Royal Naval Artificer Training Establishment. Whilst a number of other such units also bore the same name and number (namely Lympne, Sandbanks and Lawrenny Ferry), Clayton had the longest 'life' as Daedalus II. An old name in naval aviation history, Lee on Solent's HMS Daedalus (otherwise Daedalus I) was the base or headquarters of those particular units.

This then is an attempt to rediscover the story of Clayton's Daedalus II. To my knowledge, no previous attempt has been made to record this important period in North Staffordshire's history. However, the work does not claim to be a complete history of the unit, as establishments such as these tended to be set up as and when required as part of the war effort, and could be disbanded just as quickly. Furthermore, even 50 years or so after, barriers of secrecy still shield aspects of the Second World War. In addition, there were occasions when events were simply not recorded. After all, there was a war on!

Also revealed is the effect that the coming of the war, and Daedalus, had on Clayton and its inhabitants. The pre-war atmosphere of the village was never to be restored.

GB

An early photograph of Clayton Hall, with children playing on the tennis court.
Courtesy of the Headteacher, Clayton High School

Early 20th century photograph of the lodge, used as the HMS Daedalus Guardroom during World War II. The building was extended to include cells.
Courtesy of the Headteacher, Clayton High School

Chapter One
CLAYTON - THE SLEEPING VILLAGE

Today, Clayton forms part of the significant post-war urban expansion in the southern part of the Borough of Newcastle-under-Lyme in North Staffordshire. With a population of 4,280[1], many of its inhabitants commute to employment in the market town of Newcastle itself, or the Potteries and beyond. In contrast, in the 1930s, it was a village with a population of 264[2], the majority residing around The Green and in Northwood Lane. There had been little development of significance during the early part of the century with the exception, perhaps, of 'The Squares' in 1919[3] and a small estate in the 1930s, both off Northwood Lane. Moreover, unlike today, the village was separated from Newcastle by an expanse of rolling countryside which, sadly, has been subsequently lost to post-war residential development. Born in the village in the 1930s, Malcolm Williams recalls as a child standing on Clayton Road near to the Hall and 'seeing nothing but unspoilt countryside' when looking towards the town.

Until the Second World War life in the village revolved around the Hall. Built in the 1840s for the MP for Stafford Borough, John Ayshford Wise Esq., on the site of an earlier house, the property occupied a site of approx 40 acres including ornamental gardens with extensive views over Trentham, Barlaston and the surrounding neighbourhood. It was subsequently to have a number of notable occupants including the Ironmaster, Sir James Heath, but ownership eventually passed into the hands of Frederick George Johnson (1858-1923), co-founder of Johnson Brothers (Hanley) Ltd. One of the leading figures of his day in the pottery industry, Johnson was a great benefactor to the village and he and his family participated in local events, in particular the annual horticultural shows, often exhibiting their own produce. An expert horticulturalist, he built extensive greenhouses at the Hall, and was responsible for the formation of the Clayton Horticultural Society serving terms as President.[4]

After Johnson's death, the Hall passed to his widow, Charlotte. On her death in 1939, the property continued to be occupied by their spinster daughters, Florence and Dorothy, and the Johnson family remained the principal landowner in the village at the beginning of World War II. Until that time Clayton retained an atmosphere of 'rural tranquillity,' locked in a time warp. It epitomised what some might regard as a typical English village. This, no doubt, arose from the fact that the Clayton Hall Estate included a number of tenanted farms and tied cottages. Thus, the village and surroundings were predominantly agricultural[5], the main crops being oats and wheat.[6] Prior to Frederick Johnson's death in 1923 it may be said that almost every villager was employed by him, either directly or indirectly, working on one of the farms or at the Hall itself. However, upon succession to his widow, Charlotte, the number of staff at the Hall was gradually reduced. This again was the case following her death in 1939 and during the brief period of occupancy by the two daughters.

The Johnsons were regarded as good employers but, having said that, employees knew their place! Even in the 1930s when Mrs Johnson was driven into Newcastle by one of the chauffeurs, she would have been accompanied by a maid. Whilst the latter may have been overjoyed at the thought of a break from dreary household duties and an excursion into town, having arrived there, she nevertheless would have been expected to walk a few steps behind her employer. Yet another story concerns the Head Chauffeur. Arthur Frederick Herbert had gained employment with the Johnson family following his demobilisation from the RASC after World War I. He and his family resided in an estate cottage which was linked by direct telephone to the Hall. As a child, Malcolm Williams recollects visiting the house and seeing Mr Herbert snap to attention in full uniform and briskly announce 'Herbert speaking, Ma'am!' into the telephone when responding to a call from the Hall. Mr Herbert was responsible for maintenance of the Johnson's fleet of vehicles which at one time included a Sunbeam, Daimler, Rolls Royce, Alvis, Austin, Packard and a Fiat Topolino.[7] No doubt any of these would be collectors' items today had they been 'mothballed' as happened to some vehicles during the war period.

A further instance of the Johnsons in their role as benefactors relates to the Christmas parties arranged for pupils of the nearby Clayton C.P. School. Under the control of the formidable Head Teacher Miss Maudesley, the premises were situated in Northwood Lane near to its junction with Clayton Road. The party was held annually at the Hall in the pre-war years, and the routine generally followed the same pattern with Mrs Johnson initially issuing an invitation for pupils to attend. The next step was for the school to respond with a list of names and ages of pupils. On the appointed day, the children dressed in their 'Sunday best' walked from the school. Former pupil Mrs Beryl James recalls that 'the driveway to the Hall seemed endless to small legs.' On arrival Mrs Johnson, a small and frail lady, generally dressed in black, would be presented with a 'surprise' bouquet by the Head Boy and Girl. Bernard Herbert, also recollecting such events, remembers Mrs Johnson, even at his level, as 'being small' and 'smelling of mothballs!' Tea was served by the staff, following which Father Christmas (usually the Vicar of Hanford or Trent Vale!) handed out presents beneath a large Christmas tree. Games followed but many of the children wanted to ride on an old family rocking horse housed in the laundry at the rear of the Hall. This was very popular and queues generally developed. At the end of the day coats were collected and all pupils stood in line to thank Mrs Johnson for her generosity. Finally, as they left, she and a male member of staff would hand out bags of sweets and oranges.

In those far off days before World War II there were no restrictions on play areas for the children of Clayton, apart perhaps from being strictly forbidden to watch the spectacle of Yates's prize Friesian bull mating! Generally, however, they were free to wander in search of adventure. All the woods and fields were their domain and, according to Bernard Herbert, they spent 'all daylight hours out of doors.' Summers passed happily riding on hay carts, helping with haymaking and bringing cattle in for milking etc. He recalled that a 'highlight of the year' was the arrival at Yates farm of a 7-ton steam engine pulling a threshing machine which set to work in the production of sacks of grain. The machine travelled from farm to farm, creating a 'dust like fog' with all hands assisting with the strenuous work. At the end of the day the farmers' wives served pints of home brewed beer and large glasses of ice cold milk from the dairy.

During this period of the 1930s, the local embodiment of the law was Sgt Charlie Lawton who, according to Bernard, 'was always in ten places at the same time!' As with most village Bobbies, he knew everyone by name but, 'the worst thing that could happen was for Sgt Lawton to speak to one's father.' On other occasions when action was required on the part of the Sergeant, 'it was not unknown for his highly polished right boot to be planted on some offender's backside!'

The only transport that one would generally expect to see on a regular basis in Clayton in those dreamy pre-war days was farm vehicles, (mostly horse drawn), Bradley's bus or, in the better weather, Sidoli's popular bull nosed Morris ice cream van. Bradley's Tilling Stephens bus was a timber framed 1920s model which, according to Malcolm Williams,

Friars Street, Newcastle in 1937.

Author's collection

Another 1937 view of Newcastle, possibly taken from St Giles church tower. In the foreground are Old Roebuck Lane and Lower Street, with the Gas Works Retort House Tower in the background. Smithfield Cattle Market can be seen in the centre.

Author's collection

Obituary photograph of F Johnson of Clayton Hall.

Clayton Hall wearing its World War II camouflage, and the naval flag flying from the mast.
Courtesy of the Headteacher, Clayton High School

H.M.S. DAEDALUS

Courtesy of Newcastle Borough Museum

could be heard some 2-3 miles distant, warning of its approach. The distinctive whine of its engine could be heard from Hanchurch, or beyond, and this useful indicator sometimes saved waiting time at the bus stop or, alternatively, urged other intended passengers to get a move on! It was a popular mode of transport, particularly on market days when it would often be overcrowded with passengers returning with such varied items as live poultry and fruit trees. On these occasions problems would generally occur when passengers attempted to leave the vehicle, fighting their way to the exit through the inevitable mêlée! Overcrowding also caused problems as the bus attempted to climb Clayton Bank from the town. Regularly, passengers would be requested to alight and walk whilst the driver nursed the vehicle to the top, even then sometimes having to top up the radiator. But it was all regarded as good natured fun and, in a way, a social event.

This carefree and almost idyllic atmosphere, reminiscent of a H.E. Bates novel, was to continue in the village throughout the 1930s. During the long hot summer of 1939 work continued in the fields while elsewhere anxious parents put aside thoughts of Hitler and his dark forces and took their children for one final holiday. It seemed that people preferred not to think of the possibility of hostilities but on 3rd September this air was shattered by Prime Minister Neville Chamberlain's broadcast announcement of the declaration of war against Germany. Preparations for war had, in fact, begun to intrude into everyday life throughout that summer. Ration books, identity cards and public information leaflets containing such advice as 'Masking your windows,' and 'Your gas mask' appeared. Buildings found alternative service as first aid posts and, in the streets and gardens, walls of sandbags and corrugated iron Anderson shelters became familiar sights. In addition, 'blackouts' were already in place in many houses. For the children of 1939 it was an exciting period generally with gas masks requiring to be carried at all times (often along with childhood treasures!) and there were classroom competitions to see who could put them on most quickly - some were fortunate in being issued with Donald Duck or Mickey Mouse models. There was also cigarette cards to collect such as 'Aircraft of the RAF' and when war was finally declared some newspapers gave away maps of Europe with cut out flags so that families could follow the progress of the war.

One of the early casualties of the war was the popular ice cream man Mr Sidoli. Together with his counterpart Mario Togneni from Hanford, and many other highly respected citizens with a foreign background, he was classified as an alien and interned for a period at a tented camp at Prees Heath, near Market Drayton. The Government's decision to intern all aliens (ie non British) brought suffering and distress to a large number of people across Britain.[8] Many were from well established business families whose loyalties were entirely with this country. The local MP for Newcastle, Colonel J.C. Wedgwood, was one of the first in the House of Commons to draw attention to the plight of these unfortunate people and he endeavoured to ensure that they were treated fairly and with humanity.

Once hostilities began Newcastle suffered isolated raids by the Luftwaffe, the first occasion being on 14th December 1940 when a lone aircraft dropped bombs on nearby Chesterton resulting in extensive damage and numerous casualties. Subsequently, a similar incident occured on 2nd June 1941 at May Bank. But, when sirens wailed and searchlights probed the night sky the children of Clayton loved it, sensing no danger - 'excitement at last'; at least that's how the boys regarded it! The Chief ARP Warden in the village was local milkman Freddy Lindop who could often be seen walking around wearing his white tin helmet of authority. His headquarters, known locally as 'The Kremlin', was located in the cloakroom of the village school. Bernard Herbert recalls an occasion when the Warden lectured pupils on what action to take if they found unexploded bombs and anti-personnel butterfly devices. One of the class then sheepishly removed an unexploded butterfly bomb from his satchel which resulted in the Warden almost having a coronary! A few nights later a lone German raider dropped a large bomb resulting in a heavy thud which shook the whole village, but failed to explode. The Chief Warden and his colleagues carried out a thorough, but unsuccessful search for the device, during which residents were ordered to remain indoors. Three days later it revealed itself with a mighty bang causing a 40ft crater which demolished the fencing, rear garden, aviary and roof of Mr Lindop's house. As Bernard related, 'he had failed to look there!' A local farmer also lost a number of cattle when land mines exploded in the fields off Seabridge Lane and Northwood Lane. Malcolm Williams recalls seeing the carcases of a dozen or so unfortunate animals, and the huge resultant craters, some of which can still be seen today. One resident, however, observed that, on reflection, some wartime scenes at Clayton would not have been out of place in an Ealing Studio film comedy or the television series 'Dad's Army!'.

Meanwhile, across the Channel, as Hitler's Luftwaffe was revving up to unleash against Britain the type of action that it had already carried out against Spain and Poland, the petty pace of day to day living in Clayton was coming to an end. Also, air raids had occured in the Firth of Forth area of Scotland which was to have implications for the village.

NOTES

1. Figures for Clayton Ward, Borough of Newcastle-under-Lyme. March 1996
2. Census 1931
3. 'The Squares' was a development of 8 flat roofed houses (Two blocks of four). According to Newcastle Borough Council records they were built in 1919 for agricultural workers, each block having an outside water pump.
4. Sentinel 19th September 1923
5. There were 5 farms in the village belonging to Clayton Hall Estate namely, Barn, Blaggs, Chattertons, Sants & Yates. A sixth farm, Swanns, formed part of the Sutherland Estate, Trentham.
6. Kellys Directory 1940
7. Bernard A. Herbert, son of Head Chauffeur, letter to author 21st November 1994
8. The Emergency Powers (Defence) Bill, passed by both Houses of Parliament on 24th August 1939, provided measures for internment of anyone 'whose detention appears to the Secretary of State to be expedient in the interests of the public safety or the Defence of the Realm.'

Chapter Two
EMERGENCY MOVES

The first Naval Air Apprentices began training at HMS Caledonia (formerly the liner Majestic) at Rosyth, Scotland in January 1939. In the following October, the first air raid on Britain occurred, centred on the Firth of Forth adjacent to the Bridge, the Caledonia itself, the cruisers HMS Southampton, HMS Edinburgh and the destroyer HMS Mohawk. As a consequence of the raid, the apprentices were evacuated to alternative premises in Rosyth which is perhaps fortunate as, shortly afterwards, the Caledonia was destroyed by fire.

The Admiralty then decided to transfer the 80 or so apprentices to HMS Buzzard, a former civil aerodrome at Lympne on the Kent coast. Situated some 2½ miles west of Hythe, Buzzard was a Royal Naval Air Station of the Fleet Air Arm[1]. With hindsight, this would seem to have been an odd decision on the part of the Admiralty as it should have been obvious, even at that time, that the Kent coast would soon be in the 'front line!' Nevertheless, at Lympne, Lieutenant (E) Joe Haigh and WO Tom Orr set about the formidable task of building a training establishment armed with little more than 'half a Nimrod and a battered Walrus' by which time, the station had been renamed HMS Daedalus II.[2] Their labours were soon to be interrupted, however, and the 16 year old apprentices witnessed some of the results of war in the air earlier than expected.

The Air Council had already become aware of the value of this coastal air field for defence purposes and when Hitler's invasion plans became clear, two bomber squadrons under Wing Commander (later Sir) Brian Barker were transferred to Lympne[3]. The Germans had, in fact, already broken through the French frontier and were driving into the old Somme battlefields of the First World War. The swift advance seemed incredible to those who had vivid memories of the long stagnation of stationary trench warfare during the struggle of 25 years earlier. On broadcasting for the first time as Premier, Churchill, on Sunday 19th May 1940, warned that "after this battle in France abates its force, there will come a battle for our island, for all that Britain is, and all that Britain means. That will be the struggle".[4]

May 1940 saw the capitulation of Belgium and Holland, and the evacuation of British forces from Dunkirk. Spitfires filled the skies of Kent - to be joined in a few weeks by the Luftwaffe, as Germany attempted to destroy fighter stations between London and the coast, in advance of invasion.

On the same day as Churchill's broadcast, squadrons of RAF reconnaissance and bomber aircraft began arriving at Lympne and continued to do so until the hours of darkness. Numbering approximately 100, they had hurriedly evacuated from aerodromes in France with their ground crews, all of whom were badly in need of food and accommodation. Lympne airfield was put under heavy guard, and on the following day some of the aircraft were dispersed to other aerodromes.[5] Other RAF pilots were also forced to use Lympne for emergency purposes on occasion, and a number of former apprentices recollect seeing aircraft 'burning like torches and shot full of holes', limping onto the airfield from across the Channel, scenes that they are unlikely to forget.

It was against this background that the decision was taken to relocate the apprentices yet again. In any event, it had become obvious that Lympne was going to be needed by the RAF for 'operational purposes.' It is believed that, initially, consideration was given to shipping the apprentices to Canada, where they would have been able to continue training unmolested. This was certainly done to good effect later on in the war in relation to aircrews. An alternative urgent decision was taken to relocate the training establishment to Newcastle-under-Lyme in North Staffordshire. A secret schedule has survived which indicates those 'safe areas' suitable for relocation of Government Departments, but whether or not regard was had to this is uncertain. It lists a number of Shire counties which are then divided into local authority districts, and the former Stoke-on-Trent City and Newcastle-under-Lyme Borough areas are included.[6]

What does appear to be certain is that the evacuation of the training establishment (that is Daedalus II) to Newcastle-under-Lyme was instigated at the suggestion of Rear Admiral (later Sir) Denys Chester Ford, then Director of Aircraft Maintenance & Repair. The decision was taken at a hastily convened conference called to discuss the whole question of Lympne.[7] By coincidence, the Admiral was the brother of the then Mayor of Newcastle-under-Lyme, Alderman Ronald Mylne Ford, by which it is assumed that he was familiar with the town. It is also strongly rumoured that he was on friendly terms with a number of the more affluent families in the area, including the Johnsons at Clayton Hall.

Rear Admiral Sir Denys Chester Ford, who suggested relocating HMS Daedalus II to Newcastle-under-Lyme.
Courtesy National Portrait Gallery

In wartime, the tactical movement of units within a theatre is strongly influenced by events, and the actual notice given may vary from weeks to minutes. Depending upon the circumstances, the relevant orders may be passed in writing, by signal or, in an extreme case, by telephone. In the case of Daedalus II, a letter dated 23rd February 1946 from the Admiralty to Newcastle's Town Clerk confirms that the Borough was given less than 24 hours to make arrangements for the reception of the apprentices and ship's company.

Admiral Ford's suggestion to relocate Daedalus II having been endorsed, urgent signals were sent to the Mayor. Lt (E) J. Haigh (mentioned earlier) and Lt C.E. Wright left immediately for Newcastle to further advise the Mayor on their requirements, and to make arrangements for billeting, catering, and requisitioning of property under emergency powers. The Council was also informed that the first contingent would be arriving on the following day, with a likelihood of two more over the next two days.

Whilst the Mayor and the Corporation were later thanked for their 'invaluable' and 'whole hearted co-operation'[8], credit nevertheless should be given to Joseph Griffith, the Town Clerk who co-ordinated all action on behalf of the Authority which enabled the Fleet Air Arm to establish itself so quickly in the town. However, it has to be said that it was by no means a perfect operation but, given the time available and the circumstances, probably the best that could have been achieved. Griffith was a highly respected local government official, a lawyer by profession, who had succeeded his father into office. Described as an officer of 'great skill, strong character, determination and judgement,' he was the driving force behind many of the Council's major schemes of the period, including the Westlands Estate, and he gave the Fleet Air Arm and the war effort the same attention. He was certainly well known in Whitehall's corridors of power and was not averse to attending there as a one man delegation to put the Council's case, if required. During his period of office, he saw the population of the Borough increase from 20,000 to 70,000 and he was awarded the Freedom of the Borough on his retirement in 1946.[9]

With Griffith's assistance, temporary accommodation was hurriedly arranged, and a number of buildings requisitioned ready for the arrival of the apprentices and other personnel.

Meanwhile, at Lympne, verbal instructions had been received in the early afternoon of 20th May that the Fleet Air Arm was to be evacuated.[10] As a consequence, instruction of apprentices was stopped immediately and all hands turned to packing gear and equipment. Confirmation of the Admiralty message was received the following day. In the interim, rail and road transport had been requisitioned. The transfer of Daedalus II was about to get under way.

NOTES.

1. D.G.Collyer Lympne Airport in Old Photographs (1992) p8
2. The establishment was under the control of HMS Daedalus at Lee-on-Solent (otherwise Daedalus I). See also R. Sturtivant & T. Ballance The Squadrons of the Fleet Air Arm (Air-Britain 1994) p388
3. Leslie Hunt 'Lympne's war record' in Folkestone Herald 25th September 1965
4. Malcolm Thompson Churchill, his life & times (Odhams, 1965) p309
5. Captain B.L.G. Sebastian to Rear Admiral, Naval Air Stations 2nd June 1940. PRO. AIR1/10745
6. The list which has survived relates to a meeting held on 24th October 1940. However, it is evident that this, or a forerunner, had been in existence since 1938. PRO. CAB21/603-6
7. Sentinel 30th October & 14th December 1946
8. NBC. Admiralty to Town Clerk 23rd February 1946
9. Sentinel Op.cit
10. Addit. AIR1/10745

Guard at Divisions, under Lieut. Dibben, 1942. HMS Daedalus II, Clayton Hall.

Courtesy of R Kennedy

Daedalus II, Clayton. Rear Admiral Boyd taking the salute 'on the Quarterdeck' at passing out of the 1st Grenville Division Apprentices, December 1942, with the Band in the background.

Courtesy of J Fowler

Apprentices Marshall, Bear, Paige and Stiff at Lympne, (above), and Marshall, Paige and Bear at Hythe (below), in 1940.

Courtesy of L Bear.

1st Grenville Division Apprentices Clark, Harris and Kennedy at Lympne, 1940. "I look up to him ...."
Courtesy of R Kennedy.

Below:
Apprentices Lou Bear and John Stiff, messing about in boats at Hythe, 1940.
Courtesy of L Bear.

Chapter Three
THE COMING OF DAEDALUS

On the evening before the Fleet Air Arm was evacuated from Lympne, the Mayor of Newcastle-under-Lyme (Alderman R.M. Ford), via the local press, urged all to 'carry on quietly and valiantly', adding as a warning, 'but to do so we must ask for peace of mind and determination to bring our cause to a victorious end - the cause of freedom for mankind. Hard times are on us' he concluded, 'but that victory will come, let no one question'.[1]

The first personnel from Lympne arrived at Newcastle-under-Lyme railway station in the early hours of Wednesday 22nd May 1940. Surviving documents, endorsed 'Secret', reveal that the party comprised 140 apprentices and 10 Officers/Petty Officers, accompanied by 15 railway wagons of gear. At the same time a convoy of six 15 ton and two 7½ ton vehicles was heading north, under escort, with heavy stores including workshop gear, aircraft instructional frames and other technical equipment.[2]

Despite the hour, the sounds which resulted from the arrival of the Fleet Air Arm did not go unnoticed in the town. It was a warm, still night and with bedroom windows wide open, certain residents soon became aware of strange noises emanating from the direction of the railway station. Being as it was the period of Hitler's threatened invasion, some became concerned as the tramp of boots and barked orders became evident. The sounds in the night were, of course, those of the apprentices disembarking from the train. Having been cooped up for many hours during the lengthy journey from the south coast, and being totally unaware of their location, they were 'let loose', as one put it. Some were ordered to 'fall in' outside the station ready for the march into town, whereas others were directed to unload the precious equipment from the wagons. In any event, the resultant sounds were, no doubt, exaggerated, given the weather conditions and the hour.

In recalling the occasion, Mrs Sylvia Ridgway confirmed that it was their neighbour who next morning broke the news of the friendly invaders. He was a railway employee who had witnessed the arrival of the special train. Over the garden wall he informed her mother - 'The navy's arrived!' to which she responded 'Don't talk daft!' (they have a way with words in North Staffordshire!). 'It's true' he replied, but quipping 'and the Queen Mary's tied up at the Baths!' As a teenager Sylvia decided that she must go into town for a glimpse of the sailors, only to find that none were to be seen. However, there were 'a lot of young fellows hanging out of the Municipal Hall windows' she recollected, 'but they weren't wearing the customary naval apparel.' It transpired that Bert Lane, the Hall Keeper, had been called from his bed to accommodate them! Sylvia also has vivid memories of towels, tea cloths, etc, hanging from the Municipal Hall windows. 'The place was festooned as if a party was in progress - but no sailors' she recalled. Disappointed, she returned home.

Later that same day, further Daedalus personnel, including 270 Air Fitters, 36 Wrens and 20 Officers/Petty Officers left Lympne by rail bound for Newcastle-under-Lyme. Leaving at 6pm, that train also included 19 wagons of equipment. On arrival, the Wrens were housed at the Borough Arms Hotel before being eventually relocated to private billets in the Clayton area. The same arrangements were repeated on the following evening when the last of the Fleet Air Arm personnel evacuated Lympne, and the airfield was formally handed over to the RAF. This final party, some 120 in number, consisted of the remainder of the Officers and ship's company (permanent staff), accompanied by 15 wagons of equipment. Coincidentally, two 5 ton lorries containing arms and ammunition also made the journey north to Staffordshire under heavy guard, together with other transport conveying medical and dental stores. On arrival, the guns and ammunition were temporarily stored at the town's Police Station. According to a contemporary report, detraining and billeting at Newcastle 'proceeded smoothly' but entailed working most of the first three nights to ensure that urgently required wagons were unloaded, without delay, for re-use. At this stage, 600 or so personnel and 250 tons of equipment and stores had been successfully transported to the market town. The only items left at Lympne belonging to Daedalus were a number of instructional aircraft, and an urgent request for these to be transported by road was submitted.[3]

In the meantime, a number of properties had been requisitioned for use by HMS Daedalus II, which was to become known officially as a Royal Naval Artificer Training Establishment.[4] Initially, the impressive list included Old Bank House, High Street (for Captain & Commander's and Regulatory offices); Victoria House, a Nursing Home in London Road (now The Hungry Horse - for Officers' Ward Room); Westlands Girls' School (for instructional and sport purposes); Craft House, Pool Dam (for Electrical School); Smithfield Garage (subsequently Blackfriars Bakery - for Technical School/main training workshop); Blackfriars School Clinic (for sick bay & dental clinic); St Giles Parish Hall (for classroom and armoury); Burke's Higherland Garage (for workshops); Clayton Lodge (now a hotel - for Wrennery); Municipal Hostel, Holborn (now Social Services - for fitters' and certain ship's company accommodation) and, most importantly, Clayton Hall. Coincidentally, the Council's Billeting Officer and her staff were continuing to visit residences throughout the Borough area to ascertain whether there was spare capacity for accommodation, or if properties were suitable for requisitioning. Subsequently she was to report that she was experiencing difficulty in acquiring property as the Military Authorities were requisitioning all available houses in the district. As a consequence, the Council resolved that where houses were known to be available, they be 'requisitioned in advance, whether immediately required or not'[5].

Apparently, not all went well with the requisitioning of certain major properties, according to a contemporary report compiled by Major Owen Rutter for the Ministry of Information.[6] The Rector of St Giles Parish Church, Prebendary Cuthbert Watkins, registered a protest at the requistioning of his Parish Hall, whereupon he was told to 'go away and pray for peace!' It is not generally thought that the Rector wished to be seen as unco-operative or unpatriotic, but that he may have been concerned purely in relation to the use of church premises as an armoury. According to that same report there were problems at Clayton Lodge, owned by the Downing family. Here an elderly lady resisted all initial attempts to remove her from the premises, objecting to 'public requirements taking precedence over private inconvenience!' In this case the owners also objected to requisitioning on the ground that there was difficulty in rehousing their five cars! Likewise, at Clayton Hall, Misses Florence and Dorothy Johnson were, according to Major Rutter, 'ejected with difficulty'. They eventually went to live in Airdale Road, Stone, in a property they named 'Little Clayton'.[7]

The first reference in the Council records to the arrival of HMS Daedalus is on 5th June 1940, two weeks after the event. The authority continued to offer support to the establishment in various forms and this is reflected in a series of decisions recorded in the Council minutes. Work undertaken by Mr Arthur Cotton, the Borough Surveyor, is revealed, together with that of Mr S.A. Wilmot, Chief Architect of the Bourneville Village Trust, who was at the time assisting the Council with various schemes including that of the

Westlands Estate.[8] The new arrivals were also given anti-gas training by Chief Inspector Burrow and Sgt Jones of the town's Police force.[9] Moreover, arrangements for their entertainment and that of other troops in the Borough in the form of dances and concerts were approved by the Council[10] which also resolved to reduce charges to members of the Fleet Air Arm for use of the Baths.[11] Perhaps more surprisingly, the Council also generously purchased 20 volumes on aircraft maintenance and operations for the library, especially for use by the Fleet Air Arm and local Air Training Corps.[12] In addition to these facilities, a YMCA canteen was officially opened by the Mayoress, Mrs Ford, on 5th July at Higherland Chapel.[13]

In the meantime, the serious business of the taking over by the Fleet Air Arm of the various requisitioned properties was in progress. One of the first to be affected was the Westlands Girls' School. As a pupil Sylvia Mayer (now Mrs King) recollects the Senior Mistress, Miss Saunders, coming into her classroom and announcing cancellation of a hockey match to be held that afternoon and that 'the Royal Navy were taking over the school.' A further announcement that they were to transfer from their modern premises to the Victorian Hassell Street School in the town resulted in 'a series of boos' from fellow pupils. Sylvia also recalls Fleet Air Arm apprentices subsequently reporting to the school to assist with the transfer of desks and other furniture. She particularly remembers the occasion since an apprentice succeeded in dropping a desk onto her foot, a wound of which she has evidence to this day!

Naturally, some of the requisitioned buildings required major alterations to meet Fleet Air Arm requirements and these were detailed in an early secret memorandum to the Admiralty, together with a request for more transport.[14] Some of the additional work also revealed in the Council records includes the approval of plans for the erection of a temporary classroom at St Giles Parish Hall and a gymnasium at Westlands Girls' School.[15] Those same records also disclose a number of rents to be paid by the Admiralty, following consultation with the District Valuer. That of Westlands Girls' School was agreed at £1045 per annum, Friarswood School Clinic £200 p.a., and the Municipal Hostel £700 p.a.[16]

Meanwhile, ventilation in the Municipal Hall was reported as 'bad' and there was serious overcrowding with the apprentices sleeping on camp beds inches apart. There were also grossly inadequate toilet and washing facilities, which is hardly surprising as the building was not intended to be used for such purposes. To add to the problems, there was an outbreak of meningitis which resulted in 30 being segregated.[17] A number were subsequently transferred to Newcastle Isolation Hospital. Former Sick Berth Attendant Fred Lovell recalled the incident, having rendered medical assistance and also because he initially slept in the Municipal Hall. Subsequently, he slept in an old motor cycle sidecar under a staircase in the Ebenezer Schoolrooms in Merrial Street, before eventually moving 'up market' and 'to a better life' in Edward Avenue. Here he was billeted with a bank manager and his family who employed a maid. Then, as he states, he was 'waited on!' To complicate matters further from a health aspect, there was an outbreak of scarlet fever which, according to Mrs Ella Carnill, resulted in a number of apprentices being temporarily transferred to Bradwell Hospital.

The problematic situation at the Municipal Hall was eventually resolved when on 28th May all apprentices were transferred to the modern Westlands Girls' School which was said at the time to be more 'airy.' Here they slept on mattresses on classroom floors, and the washing and toilet facilities were described as 'ample'. In addition, a huge marquee was hired and erected in the school grounds, and meals were provided by a local contractor.

Meanwhile, the Admiralty had notified the Commanding Officer that the proposed total complement of personnel at Daedalus II would increase to 1,000. As a consequence, the decision was taken to accommodate all apprentices at Clayton Hall. Furthermore, Wrens would be housed at Clayton Lodge, and all other personnel billeted elsewhere. Clayton Hall had by now been vacated, and the Commanding Officer announced his intention to move some of the apprentices there by 5th June. It was estimated that, initially, 150 could be housed in the Hall itself, with 350 in hutted accommodation in the grounds.[18] Whether this target was actually achieved is uncertain.

The work to convert both Clayton Hall and Clayton Lodge to Admiralty requirements was undertaken by a consortium of local builders, namely Joseph Jones (NS) Ltd, Messrs A.V. Shenton, & Phillips Bros of Silverdale. The Hall contract also provided for construction of additional infrastructure, a number of buildings, and extensions to the lodge to form a guardroom. Meanwhile, the services of some of the Johnson family's former employees at Clayton Hall were retained, including two of the gardeners and the Head Chauffeur, Mr A.F.Herbert, all of whom lived on the estate. Mr Herbert became a uniformed driver and went on to give many years service to the Admiralty.

For the most part North Staffordshire and its people made favourable impressions on the new arrivals. With few exceptions, the Fleet Air Arm personnel were most impressed by the warmth of welcome, particularly those who happened to be accommodated in billets. Whilst this was not the case with Fred King (1st Grenville Division), he nevertheless recalls only having been in the area a few days but by which time the locals were talking to the newcomers and recommending places to visit. 'They were very friendly,' he said, 'which is characteristic of the area.' Fred, like a number of his colleagues, married a local girl and returned to live in the area after war service. Indeed, many of the daughters of the town were to take the apprentices to their hearts but, according to Sylvia King, when they first arrived, girls were 'warned not to go near them' as it was rumoured that the boys 'came from approved schools or similar establishments!' Of course, it soon became clear that this was not so.

The newcomers also came to appreciate the Staffordshire countryside, sentiments which they have retained. Some, like Fred Lovell, were also fascinated by the pits, the winding gear and slag heaps, whilst others remember the dramatic sight of the Shelton Bar steelworks at night when the sky was often reddened for miles around. According to some locals, it was possible to read a newspaper at midnight when the mighty blast furnace opened and white hot slag cascaded like lava down the waste tips. Said to have influenced the author H.G. Wells, a significant number of former Daedalus personnel recall having observed the unforgettable spectacle from the high ground of Basford where it was at its most impressive. A number also expressed how fortunate they were in their 'healthy lifestyle,' not having been employed in some of the local industries such as the mines, pot banks and later, of course, the Royal Ordnance Factory, Swynnerton.

Whilst receiving a warm welcome to the area, there were language difficulties for many. Those who originated from the north tended to fare best, but those from the south could have benefitted on occasion from a phrase book or a copy of the later classic 'Arfur Tow Crate in Staffy Cher'. As it was, they had to rely on the natives for translation - for example, 'Whut dust mane, yewth?' The new arrivals had particular difficulty in comprehending the bus conductors' destination calls such as 'Anlyonly!' (Hanley or Hanley only), and that 'duck' was a local form of endearment, such as 'dear.' Others commented that variations of the dialect in different parts of the area did nothing to aid the situation. Alf Richardson (Effingham Division) recalls being recommended to visit a certain hostelry in Boslem. Having waited at a bus stop for what seemed to have been a considerable time, he ventured to ask another intending passenger about the frequency of the buses to Boslem. He was informed that two had just gone by! Alf, by this time, had not grasped that Boslem was, in fact, Burslem! Similar difficulties were encountered with such names as Ball Green, which the locals pronounced as 'Bow Grain!'

Nevertheless, given the war situation and the urgent evacuation, it was felt that the transfer from Lympne to Newcastle had been achieved relatively successfully 'due to the hard and cheerful work of all the officers and ratings concerned,' together with the 'willing and whole hearted co-operation of the Mayor and officials of the town.' Captain B.L.G Sebastian of HMS Daedalus was soon to report that he was 'confident that maintenance ratings worthy of the Fleet Air Arm will be produced at Newcastle-under-Lyme.[19]

NOTES

1. Sentinel 21st May 1940
2. Addit AIR1/10745
3. Ibid
4. The precise date of this is uncertain, but the Admiralty was using the designation in correspondence by the end of the war, as was the local press
5. NBC. Minutes of Housing (Billeting) Sub-Committee 18th Dec 1940
6. IWM. Box 85/10/5
7. Letter from Mr C. Johnson to author 30th Sept 1996
8. NBC. Minutes of General Purposes Committee 23th July 1940
9. NBC. Minutes of Watch Committee 17th Sept 1940
10. NBC. Minutes of Council 3rd July 1940
11. NBC. Minutes of Baths Committee 11th Sept 1940
12. NBC. Minutes of Free Library Management Committee 21st Nov 1940
13. NBC. Minutes of Council 3rd July 1940
14. Captain B.L.G. Sebastian to Rear Admiral, Naval Air Stations 3rd June 1940. PRO.AIR1/10745
15. NBC. Minutes of Housing & Building Committee 10th Sept 1940 & Education Committee (Schools Management) 25th March 1941
16. NBC. Minutes of Education Committee 29th Apr 1941 and Housing & Building Committee 8th July 1941
17. Addit AIR1/10745
18. Ibid
19. Ibid

An early wartime photograph of Clayton Hall prior to camouflage painting.

Courtesy of R Kennedy.

A combined working party from HMS Daedalus after the erection of a marquee in the grounds of Clayton Hall for use as a temporary mess.

Courtesy of Mrs J Prescott

Wren stewards of HMS Daedalus, Clayton Hall 1940.

Courtesy of Mrs J Prescott

Sick Berth Attendents at Friarswood Clinic, Newcastle - one of many properties requisitioned for Daedalus II in 1940.

Courtesy of J Lovell

The former St Giles Parish Hall, Newcastle, which was requisitioned by the Admiralty for use as an armoury and classroom.

Courtesy of J Fowler

The former Blackfriar's Bakery, which was requisitioned for use as the main training Workshop/Technical School for HMS Daedalus II.

Courtesy of J Fowler

Former Craft House, Pool Dam, Newcastle, requisitioned by the Admiralty for use as an electrical school.
Courtesy of J Fowler

Below: The former Westlands Girls' School, requisitioned for instructional and sporting purposes.
Courtesy of J Fowler

The Band of HMS Daedalus, pictured with Lt. Commander Carlisle in the grounds of Clayton Hall, 1945.

Courtesy of Dave Lane.

Chapter Four
DRUMS ALONG THE LANE

The war, and the arrival of Daedalus, brought to an end the rural tranquility of the village of Clayton. Its peace was shattered by a significant increase in traffic, not only proceeding to the Hall itself, but also convoys of all types of requisitioned vehicles passing through to nearby Swynnerton where a Royal Ordnance Factory was under construction. Nevertheless, some aspects obviously remained the same. Normal work continued on the local farms and former Wrens from Daedalus recall travelling into Clayton for early morning shift work, and seeing cows returning to the fields after milking. Frequently, at that hour, the Wrens would secure a lift to Clayton on buses transporting munition workers to Swynnerton.[1]

Villagers also had to become accustomed to sounds which were otherwise alien to them following the arrival of the RNATE. In addition to being raised from their beds by a dawn chorus, or cockerel, they were treated to the distinctive sound of a bugle. Reveille was performed by a duty bugler whilst simultaneously executing a 'death defying' ride around the grounds of the Hall on a battered old bike, otherwise known as 'the red devil.' As one of the former musicians recalled - 'down the hill between the wooden huts (no brakes!), hard right at a large boulder outside the gym, and if I was still on the bike, off to the dining room for breakfast!'[2] The bugler's ride could also be hazardous from another aspect as, on occasion, pranksters would stretch a length of rope between trees in the hope of unseating the poor unfortunate individual who happened to be on duty at the time.

Duty buglers 'enjoyed' certain perks including payment of an extra seven shillings per month which then put those concerned in the monied classes. They also had an hour off work daily and would frequently participate in parades or at functions in Newcastle, after which they might be invited to attend the Mayor's luncheon. However, they admit to having sat 'well below the salt' on such occasions! At Clayton, bugles would also sound at other times of the day, and to those on duty it was a 'long bike riding, bugling day!' It was certainly not performed for job satisfaction or service to fellow man, according to Norman Mason (Effingham Division), but solely for the 'pay and perks!'[3]

The activities of one particular bugler, Harry Adams (2nd Benbow Division), have been commemorated in an ode by John White, the 'poet laureate' of Daedalus II (otherwise known as the 'Benbow Bard') -

.... Now Harry had a musical flair
Which began with a Navy bugle's blare,
In Hut 14 we could not rest
As Harry practised bugle with all his zest.

We all could see that Harry was proud,
Preparing for divisions on parade ground,
When he polished bugle to make it shine,
So the copper and brass glistened on its lanyard line.

We would all parade in our number ones
Along Clayton Hall's drive of rhododendrons,
Whilst Benbows were proud just to be there,
To hear their Harry blow his bugle with flair.

He held those notes all beautifully defined
With never a warble or any decline.
It was a musical treat to all divisions around
To hear our Harry's bugle calls, clearly resound...[4]

Naval uniforms became a familiar sight in and around the area. At Daedalus II most personnel wore peaked caps and single breasted jackets, known in naval terms as the fore and aft rig. However, there were a number of others who wore the more familiar sailors' outfits with bell bottom trousers, known as square rig. These men and the Wrens wore flat caps bearing the Daedalus name band. On other occasions, naval apprentices from the RNATE might be seen in sportswear during cross country running, or in training for other sporting events. Other more unusual uniforms were also seen at times in the area. During 1940 the villagers became accustomed to the rare sight, at least in this country, of French Foreign Legionnaires in capes and helmets on a route march from their camp at Trentham. They frequently used Northwood Lane and, in doing so, would perform some of their traditional marching songs en route.[5]

Subsequently, when hangars, classrooms and butts were erected for the RNATE on the western side of Northwood Lane, local residents were subjected to other unfamiliar sounds which today might fall under the definition of noise pollution. Live ammunition was fired from time to time in the butts but, prior to this, a naval rating armed with a megaphone would cycle along the lane warning 'firing in 20 minutes!' The purpose of this, I understand, was to prevent the inducement of a premature birth, or a heart attack!

Times being what they were, many of the RNATE personnel, particularly apprentices, could play musical instruments and at no time during its period at Newcastle-under-Lyme was HMS Daedalus II without a band. This would perform at the establishment's own parades, local events for the war effort held in the town, and civic functions such as the Mayor's parade. Moreover, the versatility of musicians was such that they were also able to perform at dances. Yet again, Northwood Lane was used for training purposes and the band, or buglers with corps of drums, would frequently march and counter-march along part of its length, to the delight of the children and residents alike. According to Malcolm Williams, the bandsmen were always well turned out, with uniforms supplemented with white belts and gaiters.[6]

When that part of the RNATE was established at Clayton Hall the entire complex was surrounded with security fencing, and sentries deployed at various points. However there were gaps, or less secure points, which the apprentices took full advantage of at times! Indeed, Bobby's Lane by the pond was a popular fraternising location with girls from the village. In general, villagers came to view the fencing as for keeping the naval apprentices in, rather than keeping the locals out! Being a training establishment, however, the residents did appreciate the purpose of the fencing, unsightly as it may have been in places. Notwithstanding, local children still found their way into the grounds during the winter for sledging on the southern slopes below the Hall and, often, they would be joined by some of the naval personnel.[7] The main entrance to the site was off Clayton Road at the former lodge. By now this had been converted to a guardroom which was always manned. There was also a secondary entrance off Clayton Lane for large service vehicles, etc.

Local people also soon grew accustomed to the sound of barked orders coming from the grounds of the Hall. This would frequently be followed by the immediate sounds of boots on gravel or tarmac as the men got 'fell in.' Similarly, they became aware of what appeared to be a foreign language - 'Lef ri, lef ri, lef ri!' which accompanied the sound of marching feet. Residents passing the guardroom on Clayton Road were also shocked, on occasion, at the manner in which an NCO would be screaming at his charges - 'You are filth! What are you? Filth will not be tolerated! Stand still when I am addressing you...!' This, together with the sight of young servicemen under punishment, doubling up and down the driveway, fully clothed and wearing a gas mask whilst simultaneously holding a rifle in the air, in hot summer conditions, caused a number to wonder what form of establishment had been thrust into their midst! Some, in any event, very much resented the intrusion of Daedalus,[8] but, on the whole, a good rapport was soon established between the naval personnel and the villagers, especially their daughters! For its part, the Royal Navy attempted to ensure that relations between the RNATE and the village were as amicable as possible with no misbehaviour on the part of the apprentices, or at least, none that was evident! To the residents, there was very little evidence in the village of any freedom for the young service personnel. Whenever they were seen there, it was always under the supervision of an NCO.[9]

NOTES

1. Mrs Joan Prescott. Letter to author. October 1997
2. Norman Mason. Letter to author. November 1997
3. Ibid
4. John White 'Harry Frederick Adams' - unpublished manuscript in author's collection. Also, letter from Mr White to author 16th April 1996
5. Malcolm Williams. Interview with author. 29th January 1998 Also, see Graham Bebbington Trentham at War (Churnet Valley Books) Chapter 5
6. Malcolm Williams. Taped interview with author. 19th February 1996
7. Ibid
8. Mrs Eileen Hicks. Interview with author. 14th September 1996
9. Malcolm Williams. op.cit

John White. the 'Poet Laureate' of HMS Daedalus II, photographed in 1947, when stationed at HMS Vulture, Cornwall.

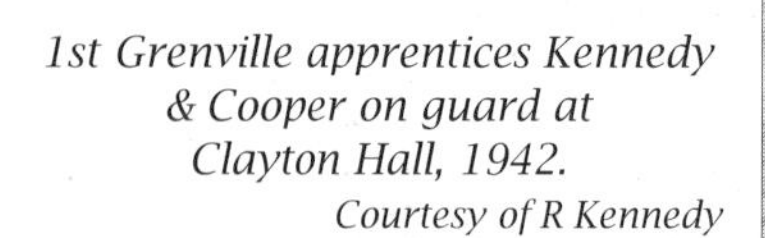

1st Grenville apprentices Kennedy & Cooper on guard at Clayton Hall, 1942.
Courtesy of R Kennedy

Interior of hut showing gear all stowed ready for inspection.
Courtesy of R Kennedy

Daedalus II, Clayton. Interior of another wooden hut, spruced up for the Commander's rounds. Each apprentice had a locker. with the standard issue blue/green suitcase stored above.
Courtesy J Fowler

A.S. Group 51. No. of Unemployment Book:- Newcastle under lyme 40394.

S. 1517 (REVISED MARCH, 1941). 90004/DS316 30m 9/42 Wt & Sons Ltd 2676/37860—672

WOMEN'S ROYAL NAVAL SERVICE.

Certificate of Service of

NAME Kathleen Mary NIXON Official No. 48572

Date of Birth 20. 12. 24

Religious Denomination Methodist

Home Address 1, The Brighton, Silverdale, Stoke-on-Trent.

National Registration Identity No. DRTG 63/3

Nearest known Relative or Friend (to be noted in pencil).

Relationship

Name

Address.

DESCRIPTION ON ENTRY

Height Feet	Height Ins.	Colour of Hair	Colour of Eyes	Colour of Complexion	Scars, Marks, etc.
5	2	Brown	Brown	Pale	None

Date of Enrolment 1 Feb. 1943. (AFO 2132/42)

Date of Commencing Duty 25. 1. 43

Period of Engagement Duration.

Establishment	Rating	Specialised or Un-specialised	Category (A.F.O. 1687/41)	Mobile or Im-mobile	From	To	Cause of Discharge
H.M.S. Daedalus II	Pro. Wren	Unspec.	General Duties	I	25/1/43	7/2/43	Enrolled
— — —	Wren	Spec.	Supply Asst. (N.S.)	I	8/2/43		Released in Class A from "HMS Godwit"

Plain clothes gratuity credited & paid in "Godwit". 22.4.46. Payment of War Gratuity & P.W.C. a

Wren Kathleen Nixon, photographed outside her parents' residence at The Brighton, Silverdale.

Chapter Five
LEARNING THE ROPES

Those joining the RNATE at Newcastle-under-Lyme quickly had to appreciate that, like all other Royal Navy shore establishments, it was considered to be a ship. Discipline was therefore maintained along naval lines. Thus, the area in front of Clayton Hall, where a flagmast was erected, became the quarterdeck. Ground beyond the boundaries of the establishment, including the guardroom on Clayton Road, was considered to be the sea! Apprentices leaving the premises would line up for inspection here before 'going ashore' and this was termed the 'liberty boat.' Those returning late were severely disciplined, the reason being that a real ship could have been under orders to sail. Therefore, any persons finding themselves in the position of having missed their ship were considered to be absent without leave (AWOL), or even deserters. Likewise, all newcomers were expected to become conversant with traditional naval terminology. Everything centred on naval terms - the deck (ground), deckhead (ceiling), bulkheads (walls), companionways (passage and stairs), the heads (toilets), stand easy (tea break), and galley (kitchen), to name but a few examples.

There is a tendency to associate Daedalus II merely with the training of apprentices. However, its responsibilities were far wider, as Air Mechanics and Fitters were also trained there. In addition, there was a large ship's company (permanent staff) of approximately one hundred and twenty personnel. Under the control of her first Commanding Officer, Captain(E) B.L.G. Sebastian, the staff dealt with the administration and day to day running of the establishment and included writers, cooks, officers' stewards, regulating staff (police), instructors, supplies & maintenance personnel, medical/dental and sick bay attendants, etc. Some of the writers, stewards and cooks were Wrens, and a number of civilians were also employed in the workshops and classrooms.

Trainee Air Mechanics and Air Fitters were either conscripts or volunteers for hostilities only. Generally, they had a trade/technical background and, once accepted into the service, had to cram an immense amount of training into a short period. When qualified, they were more likely to be immediately engaged on active service, wherever the Fleet Air Arm operated. Major Owen Rutter in a report on Daedalus II in 1942 described these particular 'older' trainees as being intended to act as a 'stop gap until the air apprentices come out in sufficient numbers'.[1] As with the apprentices, they had their own specialised branches - A (airframes), E (engines), O (ordnance (weapons)), and L (electrical/radio) and training was very intensive with progressive examinations (practical and theoretical). Courses varied in length, some being for a six month period. These trainees did not work with the apprentices, and had little or no contact with them. Some never saw Clayton Hall, or only attended there on rare occasions. Living quarters ranged from private billets to the Municipal Hostel, and pay parades tended to be at Old Bank House in town, or at the Westlands Girls' School where certain classes were undertaken.

Typical of this group of trainees, Yorkshire born John Thompson attended a radio telegraphy course at Daedalus II from June to November 1940. Prior to being conscripted, he had qualified as an electrician, but on joining the Royal Navy went on to pass a course on ship's wiring (including gunnery circuits, etc). The subsequent r/t course at Westlands Girls' School was, according to John, 'very intensive' and involved radio circuits, morse, etc. However, there was an 'air of patriotism' he recalled, with all students 'keen to do their bit' whilst at the same time wondering 'what the outcome might be'. Tradesmen such as John were urgently needed, trained as quickly as possible, and then, to quote his own words, 'thrown into the fray!' John was billeted in Milbourne Drive and, like many of his colleagues, came to love the area. Unlike some, however, being from the north, he testifies to having no difficulty in understanding the language but did notice a 'variation of dialects in different parts of the area'. After hostilities, John returned to Newcastle-under-Lyme and married a local girl.[2]

Southerner Ron Harper had completed a 7½ year mechanical apprenticeship before joining the service, and went on to attend an 18 week armament fitters course at Daedalus II. Having lost valuable time due to family bereavements in the London bombings of 1940, he nevertheless successfully gained top position on his course. During his initial period at Newcastle-under-Lyme Ron was billeted with a mining family. He recalls being fascinated that the miner worked in seams which were actually under his home, although the colliery at which he was employed was some miles away! By coincidence, Ron's father was transferred by Kodak, his employer, to work at the recently evacuated Central Clearing House at nearby Trentham Gardens. During his stay, he rented the home in Wilson Road, Hanford, of Stoke City football player Tommy Sales. Consequently, when Ron was later redrafted back to Daedalus II for a period as an instructor, he was able to reside with his family. Subsequently, he went on to serve in Malaya.[3]

Wrens also attended training courses at Daedalus II. Records indicate that in August 1942, a number were attending a course on maintenance of aerodrome defence weapons. All were said to be 'immensely keen', and their instructors spoke 'most highly' of them. A number had, in fact, already passed out earlier and been posted to air stations[4]. Whilst conscription of single women between the ages of 20-30 years (The National Service Act (No.2)) had been announced in the press in late 1941[5], large numbers of females had already left 'boring' jobs and volunteered for the services or war work. Locally, having seen the bronzed Chasseurs Alpins servicemen (the 'Beau Gestes' as they termed them!) in their midst at Trentham Park, many realised that there was more to life than counting cheques at the nearby Central Clearing House.[6] Others, like Kathleen Nixon (now Mrs Barton), preferred to join the services rather than be directed to work in a munitions factory or similar establishment. Kathleen joined the ship's company of Daedalus II on 25th January 1943, her certificate of service indicating that her engagement was 'for the duration.' Locally born, Kathleen was employed in the establishment's machine workshop, the former Smithfield Garage. Lathes and machinery were located on the ground floor, together with classrooms, and the office/stores on the floor above. Describing her workplace as having a 'happy environment', she and her colleagues were responsible for issuing tools, materials and other items to trainees. Being local and classed as 'immobile', Kathleen continued to live with her parents at The Brighton, Silverdale and commuted to work daily. Pay parade in her case was at Old Bank House in the town centre but, on occasion, she would attend at Clayton Hall for certain events. In particular, she can recall attending services at the little chapel in the grounds of the Hall.[7]

At this time women generally were, in a way, experiencing a form of liberation, a situation they would not have encountered in peace time. According to tradition, they had been raised and educated to provide children and, suddenly, they were made aware of other opportunities. Whilst many of the male population at the time may have subscribed to the view that 'you'll never win a bloody war with women in it!', they did, nevertheless, go on to make a vital contribution to the war effort.

Despite being in a reserved occupation in civilian life, former Wren PO Joyce Butcher (now Mrs Richardson) volunteered for war service in 1942. After initial training at Mill Hill, London she attended Daedalus II for an Air Mechanic electrical course. Like many others in her position, she also describes the period as one of 'intensive effort'. She and her colleagues were the first class of females to undertake the course which included such subjects as 'basic electrical instruction, workshop practice, wiring up boards, battery charging, the 'wondrous' workings of generators and commutators and the electrics of a Swordfish aircraft'. Tests were held weekly to ensure students were up to standard, with the final examination at the end of the six month period.

Joyce recalls that there were about ten other classes of 'matelots' at Craft House, Pool Dam (subsequently Garner's premises and now demolished) and so she and her fellow Wrens were a 'great attraction to the men, no doubt taking their minds off their work.' In the meantime the powers that be decided that the male trainees in the building should not mix with the newly arrived females during 'stand easys' (break periods). Consequently, the Wrens were given priority and allowed out first into the courtyard, whereupon the males would 'hang out of the windows all the time.' When a bell eventually sounded for the Wrens to return to class, yet another sounded subsequently for the males to be unleashed and the 'thunder of their boots racing down the stairs to the courtyard made any resumption of instruction from our PO teachers impossible'. It seemed that their departure from the building made it 'shudder and sway' she recalls.[8] John Fowler (2nd Benbow Division) also attended lectures in the old building, a former mill, and remembers that there were gaps between floorboards, such that one could hear the lecture in progress on the floor below.[9] Joyce's six month course also involved classes at the Westlands Girls' School where subjects such as maths and algebra were taught. Drill (square bashing) was also performed here. On occasion classes would be visited by top brass. Joyce recalls that when this occurred, someone would appear at the door of the classroom and mutely warn that they were about to arrive by putting his/her right hand from wrist to elbow thus indicating that the visiting VIP was someone with an amount of gold braid! Joyce was billeted with a colleague in what she describes as a 'tweeny two bedroomed little house' with a family who had just had a baby. By this time she writes, 'England was well into rationing, and one really wondered how our landladies cheerfully managed to feed us'.[10]

Former Leading Wren Mrs P. Casewell remembers her time at Newcastle 'with great affection.' Having spent an obligatory two week period at Mill Hill, London, she joined HMS Daedalus II on 13th January 1943 to be trained as an Air Mechanic (Ordnance). She particularly recalls CPO Tim Gavin who treated her and her colleagues in 'a jocular father like manner' whilst at the same time 'demanding high standards'. There was also a gentle quiet civilian instructor, a Mr Fitzgerald, who was 'treated with great respect'. 'Working on a Walrus aircraft, loading and arming bombs, and servicing the bomb racks fitted beneath the wings formed part of the training', she recollects. She also became familiar with handling, loading and servicing Browning ·303, ·5 Vickers gas operated and Hispano 20mm guns, thanks to 'excellent instructors'.[11] Aged between 18-20, fourteen girls successfully completed that particular course.

Among the instructors were highly experienced personnel, specialists in their field, who had remained in the service having made their way up from the lower deck. They were much respected officers who understood the young apprentices and could handle them much better than their civilian counterparts who had been drafted in from grammar schools, etc. Alf Richardson (Effingham Division) recalls the time when he and his colleagues were introduced to Lt (E) R.G. Swift who taught workshop technology at the main training workshops (ie former Blackfriars Garage). Before introducing his young charges into the art of how to use the Challenger lathes and how to make their own lathe tools, he held up his hands in the air and said 'these will earn you a living, and I will teach you how to use them!' According to Alf, 'he did. He was a good teacher and highly respected officer'. Many other instructors were former service personnel recalled to the colours and varied in rank. As the war progressed, however, some former apprentices like Jack Carnill (1st Benbow Division), having qualified, and perhaps having had some experience at sea or with a squadron, found themselves redrafted back to Daedalus II as instructors.

From time to time such staff would be supplemented with others who would arrive to deliver specialist lectures. Notable amongst these was the BBC newsreader Bruce Belfrage. Belfrage became famous when his distinctive voice became familiar to radio listeners during the early dark days of the war. On one occasion, 15th October 1941, a bomb struck Broadcasting House whilst he was reading the news. Seven of the staff were killed and the explosion was clearly heard on air, but Belfrage continued reading after only a slight pause.[12] In 1942 he left the BBC and obtained a commission in the Special Branch of the RNVR (Naval Intelligence). His job consisted largely of lecturing on a wide range of subjects concerning 'security, escape, interrogation and Japan.'[13] It was in this capacity that Belfrage visited Clayton Hall. John White (2nd Benbow Division) recalls the occasion when Belfrage addressed his division in the canteen on what to do if they were captured by the enemy. When he came to advising them on what to do if they were taken prisoner by the Japanese he remarked, according to John, 'God help you!' Belfrage then completed his lecture by talking about his former work at the BBC.[14]

As the war progressed, some instructors arriving at Daedalus II had experienced action and turned out to be highly decorated. CPO Harry Gregg had just been awarded the Conspicuous Gallantry Medal when the destroyer in which he was serving, HMS Glowworm, had been in action against the German cruiser Hipper. CPO Kenneth R.James had also seen action in the Malta convoys. Frequently, such personnel were detailed to give talks on their experiences to the young apprentices, but none enjoyed performing this task.[15]

Former Wren Irene Clifford was transferred to the ship's company from Chatham in 1943. Sleeping in a bunk in the Clayton Lodge ballroom, she cooked for her colleagues billeted there. Subsequently, she was moved to Victoria House, London Road, Newcastle (now the Hungry Horse restaurant but affectionately known as Vicky House by the Wrens) which served as the Officers' Wardroom. On one occasion the Captain and his wife were entertaining guests at a meal for which Irene had prepared a bread & butter pudding. Afterwards, she was admonished for not having included sufficient fruit in the ingredients. But it was 1944 and due to the war and rationing, etc, no dried fruit was available! However, this was the only time that she was in trouble, she recalled. She has fond memories of the area, and she particularly remembers Trentham Gardens. As a Yorkshire lass, her accent caused amusement among the locals, but she made many friends. Subsequently, on VE Day, they sang 'On Ilkley Moor Baht'At' for her.[16]

For instructional purposes, Daedalus II had a variety of aircraft initially housed at the Westlands Girls' School and Higherland Garage. Later, in 1943, the Northwood Lane hangars were built, whereupon all aircraft were transported there. In the beginning, the establishment had a Swordfish, a Skua, a Fulmar, a Proctor and a Martlet. According to a British Aviation research document a Shark, an Albacore, a Tiger Moth, a Spitfire, a Walrus and a Hurricane were subsequently added.[17] On the other hand, Kenneth James, a CPO Instructor at Clayton in 1945, also remembers a Seafire, a Mustang and a Barracuda being present at Northwood Lane.[18] In addition to the aircraft, a Bolton & Paul hydraulic gun turret was in use at the establishment's armoury in the Parish Hall.

There are locals of a certain age group who remember seeing some of the Daedalus aircraft of the period, particularly the Martlet as it was located on the front of the Westlands Girls' School initially. John Edwards also recalls aircraft housed for a period at Higherland Garage. As a child in the Poolfields area of the town, he lived near to the premises. A neighbour happened to be friendly with one of the Fleet Air Arm apprentices who, at times, had to undertake fire watching duties at the garage. When such occasion arose, John would be requested to take a flask of tea and sandwiches to him. As a reward, John would be allowed to sit in the cockpit of the aircraft and, for a while, he was 'Biggles winning the war!' Describing events a half century or so later, John says it is something that he is unlikely to forget. To a ten year old it was 'a marvellous and unbelievable experience.'[19]

Malcolm Williams also recalls the aircraft at the Northwood Lane hangars. They could be viewed by sitting on nearby fencing. However, he and his chums were not allowed to sit there when the aircraft guns were being fired into the butts.[20] Don Drayton (Raleigh Division) recounted his experiences of being trained there to line guns and maintain them, constantly taking them apart and rebuilding them. Live ammunition was also fired into the butts after appropriate warnings to residents.[21] Similarly, apprentices worked on engines at the premises, constantly removing them from aircraft, reinstating them, and running them on test.[22]

NOTES

1 IWM. Box 85/10/5
2. John L. Thompson. Interviews with author 14th September & 31st October 1996
3. Ron Harper. Telephone interview with author 12th May 1996, letter to author 21st October 1996
4. Addit. IWM. Box 85/10/5
5. Sentinel 2nd December 1941
6. Graham Bebbington Trentham At War (Churnet Valley Books) p63
7. Mrs K. Barton. Interview with author 8th August 1996
8. Mrs J. Richardson. Letter to author 25th January 1998
9. John Fowler. Telephone interview with author 13th September 1996
10. Mrs J. Richardson. Op.cit
11. Mrs P. Casewell. Letter to author 4th May 1996
12. Obituary in Daily Telegraph 16th August 1974 & The Times 17th August 1974
13. Bruce Belfrage One Man In His Time (Hodder & Stoughton) pp 135/7
14. John White. Letter to author 4th May 1996
15. Kenneth R. James. Letter to author 12th April 1997
16. Mrs Irene Clifford. Letters to author 2nd June & 15th July 1997
17. Royal Navy Instructional Frames (British Aviation Research Group) p12
18. Kenneth R. James. Op.cit
19. John Edwards. Interview with author 14th September 1996
20. Malcolm Williams. Taped interview with author 19th February 1996
21. Don Drayton. Interview with author 18th September 1996
22. Kenneth R. James. Op.cit

Wireless Telegraphy Course personnel, taken in 1940 at Westland Girls' School, one of many buildings requisitioned by the Admiralty for Daedalus II. This picture was loaned by John L Thompson, third from the left, back row.

Cooks and Stewards of HMS Daedalus II, Clayton Hall, October 1944.
Mrs I Lancaster (née Camm), who supplied the photograph, is first on the second row.

CPO Tim Gavin, who did so much to enrich the social life both at the HMS Daedalus II base and in the area generally.

Courtesy Ken Gavin

Former BBC newsreader Bruce Belfrage - a photograph taken in 1943 when he was serving with naval intelligence.

Lieut (E) R G Swift, who taught workshop technology at Daedalus II. This photograph was taken in the 1930s, when Lieutenant Swift was serving in China.

Courtesy G W Swift

Air fitters on an armament course at HMS Daedalus II in 1940. Ron Harper, who supplied the photograph, is seated third from left, front row.

Wrens Bannister, Oughton and Butcher, with male colleagues, HMS Daedalus II, 1942.
Courtesy Mrs J Richardson

Stores and office staff outside the Smithfield Workshops (now Burgess's Bakery) in 1945.
Back: PO Rowel, LSAs Hughes, Wells and Galloway.
Front: Wrens Nixon, Shaw, Alexander and Lowry. The child is Susan, daughter of P O Rowel.
Courtesy Kathleen Nixon

Cricket team, HMS Daedalus II, Clayton 1944.

Courtesy Head Teacher, Clayton High School

2nd Grenville Division Gym team, 1943/44, HMS Daedalus II, Clayton Hall. John Williams, who kindly supplied the photograph, is 2nd left, front row.

Chapter Six
APPRENTICES ON THE QUARTERDECK

The majority of the FAA apprentices at Newcastle-under-Lyme came from working class families in naval towns such as Plymouth, Portsmouth, Chatham, Sheerness or Rosyth. In addition, many had naval parentage or connections. Their families had experienced the 1926 General Strike with the subsequent poverty and deprivation of the 1930s, and they were accustomed to a strict home life and school discipline which some today might regard as harsh. Consequently, to be accepted as an apprentice and then being fed, clothed (albeit in a uniform) and to sleep in one's own bed/bunk was regarded as a luxury! Thus, apprenticeships were highly sought after. Entrance was via a Civil Service examination and of the 1,000 who undertook the June 1939 session, only 200 were selected.[1] Medical examinations followed before final acceptance. Whilst many of the boys came from grammar schools, few parents could afford 6th form education, and university was generally out of the question. But, in any event, in the naval towns, it is true to say that boy pupils were groomed for the Civil Service examinations, for achieving an apprenticeship in the RN/FAA or dockyard was regarded as a job for life.

Some of the boys came to the RNATE at Newcastle-under-Lyme having just progressed into long trousers. Many hadn't started shaving. Within a short time, however, they were rubbing shoulders together, swearing and shaving, and were starting to become men, or so they thought! During the impressionable years of their training, they were each others' closest and strongest influence and they bonded together in their individual training divisions with exceptional allegiance and esprit de corps which has lasted the years. As Ray Kennedy (1st Grenville Division) reflected - 'there is something about living together, being dependent on one another, and helping one another, that engenders a very good spirit'.[2]

Some came to acquire strange names such as 'Moose' Almond, 'Tupp'ny' Rollo, 'Moogy' Morgan, 'Buzz' Budden, 'Chick' Fowler, 'Stagger' White, 'Rover' Dover, 'Gig' Puttock, 'Oscar' Newnham, 'Stumpy' Lewis, etc. Names to conjure with, or, as one former apprentice observed, 'all worthy of a Steinbeck novel!' However, similar names also applied to some of the instructors (although certainly not to their faces!) - 'Killer' Kent, 'Cossy Motto', 'Full-A-Bull', 'Spit Whit', 'Gillie' Potter, etc.

In the RNATEs, apprentices were regarded not so much as junior ratings but more as CPOs under training. This was not only on account of their lengthy academic, professional and craft training but also due to their character development. Training was for a specific trade - A (airframes), E (Engines), O (Ordnance) and L (electrical/radio). In addition, whatever their specialisation, the boys received training in basic engineering practices and normal school subjects such as maths, English, etc. There were also current affairs lectures, military training and seamanship together with a great emphasis on sport. Life resembled that of a very disciplined school and a naval/military academy. As John Hale (2nd Benbow Division) comments in his book 'The Grudge Fight', 'thrust into a man's world, they had to exchange the undisciplined diversity of their previous lives for the clear cut authoritarian uniformity of the service'.[3] Thus many have referred to the training schemes as 'Whole Man Apprenticeships'. They were certainly successful, so much so that, when former apprentices came to leave the service, they were much sought after by industry.

Pay for a first year apprentice in 1939 was five shillings and three pence per week. Of this he received two shillings, paid fortnightly. The remainder was 'put aside' for laundry, boot repairs, replacement clothing and leave cash. Rail travel was free. At the beginning of hostilities, the normal length of apprenticeship was three years. If successful, apprentices would then pass out as an Air Fitter. One year later, they were able to qualify as a Leading AF, whilst after a further twelve months they could achieve the rank of Artificer 4th Class (or PO). However, these Regulations were to alter towards the end of the war.

The route for an apprentice to the RNATE, Clayton Hall, was likely to be achieved by various means, dependent upon chosen trade, and the circumstances prevailing at the time of hostilities. In August 1939 Jack Carnill's training division (1st Benbow) reported to Victory Barracks, Portsmouth, for initial military training (square bashing, etc) and kitting out. A training division normally comprised 150-190 boys who would at this stage be divided into their trade groups. From Portsmouth, Jack was drafted to RAF Cosford and then RAF Halton where he and those of his colleagues who had chosen ordnance (armaments) as their speciality received their next stages of training. Others from the division who had chosen engines and air frames went to RAF Hednesford, whilst electrical apprentices went to Rosyth. After a year they all transferred to Clayton Hall for their final two years of advanced training.[4] In complete contrast, Tony Creasy and his colleagues of 1st Anson Division did their initial training at a former holiday camp near Ryde on the Isle of Wight. From there they were drafted to Clayton where they undertook their full three years apprenticeship.[5] Later on, divisions reported to HMS Daedalus I, Lee on Solent, and received initial training at nearby Seafield Park. Thence, dependent upon trade, they arrived at Clayton from either Rosyth or Torpoint.

A typical day for apprentices at HMS Daedalus II is illustrated by the following:-

0630hrs	Reveille! Wash/shave, make bed, etc.
0700-0730hrs	Breakfast.
0745hrs	Fall in. Inspection and morning prayers.
0755hrs	March into Newcastle or to Northwood Lane for classes.
1000-1010hrs	Stand easy. Issued with milk and soft roll. Return to class/workshop until -
1200 noon	Transport to Clayton for lunch, those at Northwood Lane would march to the Hall.
1300hrs	Return to classes etc by transport to town or on foot to Northwood Lane.
1630hrs	March back to Clayton Hall.
1700hrs	Tea.
1830hrs	Supper and/or first 'liberty boat' ashore if free from studies or duty watch.

It should be noted that the march to and from Newcastle was completed in any weather. As a concession, however, transport was provided at lunchtimes only, to enable the apprentices to have a reasonable length of lunch break. Also, some evenings were not free, but given to studies at the Westlands Girls' School premises.

Interspersed with study and practical training there were periods of physical training in the well equiped gymnasium. John White (2nd Benbow) remembers having to climb a rope up to the roof, then turn upside down and descend with arms outstretched and the rope 'locked between one's feet and legs'. Whilst there were many fine gymnasts at Clayton a number, nevertheless, 'suffered a nasty cropper' according to John! All had to participate in boxing, and some from Clayton went on to represent the Royal Navy in the inter-services contests. Other sporting activities included football, hockey, cricket, rugby and cross-country running.[6] Swimming was pursued at Newcastle's King George V Memorial Baths and/or Trentham Gardens where there was also rowing in Admiralty cutters and whalers.[7]

Inter division competitions were also held and strongly contested, and in 1944 the 2nd Benbow Division succeeded in winning every trophy at the establishment.[8]

The RNATE, including Wrens, also participated in sports competing against local teams, an activity regarded as a goodwill gesture and another way of mixing into the community. Amongst others, assorted competitions were held against staff of the Central Clearing House at Trentham, particularly hockey.[9] But Dave Lane (Hood Division) recollects some of his colleagues helping Staffordshire to win the County Youth Football Cup at the old Stoke City football ground in 1943.[10] Another event worthy of mention is a football match against Robinson's FC which resulted in a resounding victory for a team from Daedalus. In the first game of the 1944-45 season, the Fleet Air Arm won by 21 goals to nil! Composed of workers from G.A. Robinsons of Hartshill, the opposing team nevertheless went on to be Newcastle League champions in the following season![11]

Whilst boxing was encouraged, fighting amongst boy entries or apprentices was forbidden. The Royal Navy, however, combined its prohibition with a permissive remedy. If two boys (or men) wished to fight each other, they had to go before an officer who arranged a match for them under proper supervision. This was termed a 'Grudge Fight'. Otherwise, fighting was an offence which carried severe punishment. John Hale (2nd Benbow Division) wrote a remarkable novel on the subject about such an encounter at a wartime RNATE where boy entries were 'physically and mentally conditioned to the total world of the service'. A number believe that the book is based on the writer's time served at Clayton, but he states otherwise, contending that it was based on his earlier experiences at the RNATE, Torpoint.[12] On hanging up his uniform, John Hale went on to write a number of books, but no other refers to time spent in the service. He is a former Director of the Bristol Old Vic, and recently was screenwriter for the television adaptation of Joseph Conrad's 'Nostromo'.

The apprentices received six weeks leave entitlement, generally three in the summer, two at Easter, and one at Christmas. If any boy failed part of an end of term examination, he was given extra study in his all too sparse spare time. Alternatively, if he failed badly, he was 'back classed' which was regarded as a great dishonour, seniority being all important. Failing on a second occasion was likely to result in dismissal from the service.

NOTES

1. Anon. Letter to author 4th December 1996 (correspondent, a retired naval officer who was successful in passing that session's examinations, wishes to remain anonymous)
2. Ray Kennedy. Tape of memories of HMS Daedalus II, November 1996 (author's private collection)
3. John Hale. The Grudge Fight (Collins) Cover note
4. Jack Carnill. Interviews with author 30th October 1996 and 18th February 1998
5. H.F. Creasy. Letter to author 7th May 1996
6. John White. Letter to author 16th April 1996
7. Don Drayton. Interview with author 18th September 1996
8. John White. op.cit
9. The Outcast (CCH magazine) Bound volume II covering 1941/42 period. pp 300 & 338
10. D. Lane. Letter to author 15th January 1998
11. Roy F. Briscoe in The Way We Were November 1997 p11
12. John Hale. Letter to author 15th March 1997

Anson Division Football XI, Daedalus II, Clayton 1940-43
Back: D Lambert, R Fletcher, F Pring, W Watson, P Tracy, W Barn, R Jackson
Front: H Creasy, P Chase, Lt Commander Rothwell, E Tucker (Capt), P T Jones, A Still, V Jones.
Courtesy H Creasy

Anson Division Hockey XI, Daedalus II, Clayton 1940-43
Back: J Smith, G Horton, J Steohens, J Grant, K Ellis, H Field, J Horley
Front: P Tiley, C Allen, Lt Com. Rothwell, H Creasy (Capt), P T Jones, G Gurney, C Wigmore
Courtesy H Creasy

Chapter Seven
ON BOARD AT CLAYTON

In the early years of hostilities, the requisitioned Clayton Hall and its environs gradually became transformed to fulfill their role as an integral part of the RNATE, HMS Daedalus II. With a White Ensign flying from a flag staff in front of the Hall main entrance, the site soon began to take on the appearance of a naval establishment. Furthermore, being wartime, the main building itself was camouflaged.

The first apprentices to arrive at Clayton were accommodated in the Hall with 'every inch of space' being utilised, according to a number of correspondents. Other accommodation in the main building included a recreation room in the large conservatory, and the Regulatory Office on the ground floor. In addition, a small NAAFI shop occupied part of the entrance, staffed by two 'very attractive' local girls. On occasion, they would tend to 'decorate' the Hall entrance behind the Commander as he took the salute at parades, and some of those in the ranks found this very distracting![1] Subsequently, when the apprentices were able to be accommodated in wooden huts in the grounds, the Commmander and a number of senior officers had offices in the Hall where they also slept. Other officers continued to reside at Victoria House in the town.

With a capacity of 18, including a PO apprentice, the wooden huts were used to house the junior training divisions. Bunks were arranged around the walls, with a stove and lockers occupying space in the middle of the room. Black out curtains were fitted to the windows. Toilets and washrooms were in adjoining huts and reached via duckboards in all weathers. Despite a coal and coke shortage, occupants always seemed to be able to wangle a supply, even if it was gained by raids on adjoining huts. Nevertheless, former residents recall that the accommodation was very cold in the winter, despite the stoves being stoked until they were 'white hot'![2]

By late 1942 most of the work required by the Admiralty had been completed, the architect being Mr George Greaves. Three local firms had initially been engaged to carry out the contract, but two of these, Messrs A.V. Shenton and Phillips Bros, subsequently left the site prematurely to undertake other work. According to Harry Jones, who acted as site agent, the contract was eventually completed by Joseph Jones (NS) Ltd.[3]

It is difficult to indicate precisely when certain phases of the contract were completed, but a surviving report of 1942 indicates that a dual purpose gymnasium had recently been erected, together with a chapel, canteen and messdecks. The report also confirms the existence of eight brick built dormitories to accommodate the senior training divisions. Known as the 'P' huts, these were also intended to serve as air raid shelters, having a concrete reinforced roof.[4] Jack Carnill (1st Benbow Division) recalls that there were problems for occupants of these in the form of severe condensation. Also, in the winter, it was not unknown for boots to freeze to the floor! There was one advantage, however, in that occupants did not have to leave the building for ablutions![5]

By this time a sick bay had also been provided on site. Sick Berth Attendant Fred Lovell described the building as 'a small, windowless bomb shelter with air locks, containing emergency gear with basic first aid equipment'. Whilst Fred was normally employed at the establishment's main clinic at Blackfriars, he and his colleagues nevertheless had to visit the Clayton Hall sick bay on a regular basis as duty attendant. He recalls an unforgettable occasion when he had to spend the night in the tiny building in the presence of a corpse! Fred married a local girl and he and his wife Dorothy also made history when their son Anthony was the first to be christened in the newly erected chapel by the Naval Chaplain Rev R.B. Feast MA, in August 1943.[6]

In addition, when completed, the site included ship's company accommodation in the form of Nissen huts, stores and a large garage which could also serve as a covered parade ground. Surviving records show the Wrennery at Clayton Lodge was completed by August 1942 and describe it as 'very comfortable'.[7] Also, by such time, the unit's main telephone exchange was fully operational at the converted former chauffeur's cottage at the junction of Clayton Road and Seabridge Lane.

The final piece of the Daedalus II jigsaw was the completion in 1943 of the instructional buildings in Northwood Lane comprising hangars, classrooms and firing butts. Mrs Eileen Hicks recalls these being erected, and the buildings then being painted by a team of female operatives.[8]

With the completion of the works at Clayton, and taking into consideration the numerous requisitioned premises, it can be seen that the land eventually held for HMS Daedalus II resulted in the Admiralty controlling major land holdings at Newcastle-under-Lyme. Thankfully, however, despite all the major works which had been carried out at Clayton Hall, the renowned rhododendrons and azaleas remained, together with large numbers of trees and shrubs which had been planted by the Johnsons and earlier owners.

NOTES

1. Anon. op.cit
2. John White op.cit
3. Harry Jones. Letter to author 13th June 1996
4. Report of Major O. Rutter. IWM Box 85/10/5
5. Jack Carnill. Interview with author 30th October 1996
6. Fred & Dorothy Lovell. Interview with author 12th November 1996
7. Major O. Rutter op.cit
8. Mrs E. Hicks. Interview with author 14th September 1996

Daedalus II, Clayton. A wartime photograph showing the PO Apprentices' Rest Room, centre foreground, with the entrance to Hut 16 left and entrance to Hut 1 to the right.

Courtesy J Fowler

Daedalus II, Clayton. A rare view taken during the winter of 1942, looking towards the Gymnasium, with Huts 9-16 on the left and Huts 1-8 on the right.

Courtesy J Fowler

Former Chapel of HMS Daedalus II in 1996. The building is now used for storage purposes by Clayton High School.

Author's collection

HMS Daedalus II.
Service accommodation (P Huts), photographed from Clayton Hall, with the hall gardens in foreground.

Courtesy Head Teacher, Clayton High School

1992 - Two views of 'P' Huts - former HMS Daedalus Buildings at Clayton, just prior to demolition.
Courtesy Newcastle Borough Council

Hook Boys (CPO & PO Apprentices) of Hood and Raleigh Divisions. HMS Daedalus, with Clayton Hall in the background, 1945.
Courtesy Dave Lane

Chapter Eight
FLOGGINGS AND JANKERS

Discipline at HMS Daedalus II was conducted in accordance with King's Regulations and the Naval Discipline Acts since the premises formed part of the Royal Navy. The establishment was run along the lines of a military academy and a *very* disciplined school. Evidence of this can be gleaned from the Navy List (Officer Class) for Daedalus II which includes the posts of Headmaster Lieutenant and schoolmasters in addition to ordinary instructors.

Discipline was, and had to be, strict, but as may be expected, former apprentices have varying opinions as to the level experienced. Some described life at Clayton as 'tough', 'brutal', and 'not much fun!' On the other hand, a number having arrived at Clayton from the 'military machine' at Rosyth, thought discipline much slacker. Rosyth was said to be one of those establishments where one 'saluted anything that moved and whitewashed anything that didn't!'

Cleanliness and dress were considered to be of great importance. Insubordination, slackness, late return from shore leave, improperly dressed, inattention in the classroom, etc, were amongst those offences which led to being put on 'Commander's Report.' Likely retribution (known as '8A punishment') would be several days of jankers (services slang for extra drill and work). The drill was usually of an arduous nature - doubling (running at the double) in cold or warm weather in full kit, often wearing a gas respirator whilst holding a rifle with both hands above the head or, even more traumatically, 'frog marching up an incline!' Extra work normally involved cleaning duties. In addition, offenders took their meals at a 'special 8A table' in the dining hall, so that they could be seen by all to be under punishment. Understandably, this was said to be very effective as a deterent.

More serious misdemeanours, outright insurbordination, stealing and suchlike offences, were punishable by the birch. This was a wooden rod or bamboo cane approximately 24"-30" in length. The offender, dressed in a white duck suit, was paraded before the entire ship's company and the charge would be read out by the Commander. The requisite number of strokes or lashings was then administered by the Master at Arms, the offender being held down by the legs and arms bent over a gymnasium wooden horse or similar. If the punishment drew blood, salt was applied to the wounds, usually after examination by the Medical Officer. Application of salt in itself was quite painful, but it was said to disinfect and heal the wound. Again, the fact that the punishment was carried out in front of the ship's company was perhaps the most painful part of the procedure, and the greatest incentive to avoid a recurrence. On the other hand, in certain instances, displaying wounds from such punishment had the effect of turning some into heroes.

For even more serious breaches of conduct, such as indecency, one could be 'drummed out' of the service in disgrace. A former apprentice recalled having witnessed such an occasion at Clayton. All divisions lined the driveway with the defaulter being escorted between the ranks in a slow march with a drummer tapping out a staccato beat. As he proceeded along the drive, all his badges of rank and buttons were ripped from the uniform until he eventually arrived at the guardroom on Clayton Road 'looking like a tramp'. The offender was then returned to custody until he could be formally dismissed the service, still in his 'tatty' clothes.[1]

Living in such an environment, it is perhaps not surprising that some personnel, particularly the younger apprentices, found themselves under a certain amount of stress. Reasons for this included:–

i) overwork from studies during the period in which they were coincidentally being physically and mentally conditioned to the total world of the service.
ii) the bullying attitude of certain P.O. Instructors, some of whom were 'hard characters.'
iii) being away from home and family for the first time, and being unable to adjust to the service life and/or get on with colleagues.
iv) concern for their families, particularly those living in the capital or southern naval towns which were constantly being bombed. Indeed, a number of apprentices lost members of their families and their homes following raids by the Luftwaffe. Others lost parents or relations in the general theatre of war.

At this time there were no stress counsellors as such. However, to alleviate the situation, anyone suffering from such symptoms would be counselled or interviewed by the Medical Officer. But, according to former Sick Berth Attendant Fred Lovell, this would generally be of the 'pull yourself together' approach.[2]

An example of the type of stress being experienced by some of the younger personnel may be illustrated by the case of Ron Harper who attended Daedalus II on an 18 week armament fitter's course. During this period his sister died in the London Blitz and a request on compassionate grounds to attend her funeral was refused. As a consequence, Ron 'jumped' ship to enable him to be present with his family at the internment. However, whilst in London, he presented himself to the Lords Commissioners at the Admiralty who granted him 5 days leave, after which he returned to Newcastle-under-Lyme.[3] Another tragic incident involved an apprentice who lost his entire family when their Portsmouth air raid shelter received a direct hit from a German bomb. On another occasion, an apprentice lost his father, a serving officer, when he was killed by friendly gunfire during an exercise on Salisbury Plain[4]. Thus, the personnel of Daedalus II may have been relocated from the 'front line' but there was no escape from the contingencies of war.

Divisional Petty Officers governed the lives of the apprentices. They were assisted by Chief PO & PO apprentices (prefects, also known as 'Hook Boys'), specially selected personnel from Senior Divisions who, according to some, were 'gifted at just about everything'. The CPO apprentices wore a gold chevron and star on each cuff, whilst the PO apprentice wore a similar badge on the left cuff only. Generally, all members of staff had authority over the boys. Therefore, the best policy was to say 'Sir!' (and act accordingly) to 'just about anything that moved!' 'Fagging' for PO apprentices was also not uncommon.

Naturally, there are varying opinions on the officers of the establishment, a number of whom had been recalled to the colours. Some were regarded as 'father-like' figures and who could impose discipline in a humane manner. In complete contrast there were some younger officers whom, it is alleged, 'lied' to the authorities to substantiate certain charges, resulting in unjust punishment. Others were regarded as nothing less than a 'nasty piece of work', even 'sadists!' Furthermore, a number of officers appeared to resent the task that they were performing, giving the impression that they 'hated' their protegies/pupils, regarding them as 'the lowest form of life!'

When returning from 'shore leave', apprentices had to ensure that they were not late, especially when certain officers were in charge of the guard. One fastidious officer was renowned for having a countdown for those waiting for admittance at the guardroom. At the given hour he would proceed down the line pointing to individuals and loudly counting '5 - 4 - 3 - 2 - 1, after which all were classed as late and put on report. The fact that many had arrived on time had no relevance! Consequently, apprentices were regularly seen running in groups up Clayton Bank and along the main road at great speed despite, at times, having consumed samples of the local ale. On occasion they would be accompanied by their girlfriends, as they didn't have the time to take them home. The velocity at which they ascended the bank and proceeded along the main road to 'beat the clock' is still recalled, and admired, by those locals of a certain age group today. As one former apprentice quipped - 'Roger Bannister never broke the record for the 4 minute mile!'[5]

One PO appeared to be obsessed with cockroaches. Whether or not this was purely from an environmental health aspect is unclear! On occasions that he was Duty Officer, members of the picket would be detailed to arm themselves with vacuum cleaners and report to the galley. Here, the machines would be switched on and the Duty Officer in question would turn off the galley lights for a short period. On the order 'NOW!' the lights would be turned on and the suction pipes of the machines hurriedly passed over the cooking ranges to collect the offending creatures![6]

Another eccentric character was a Yorkshire born PO who was frugal to excess. Recalled to the colours, this particular officer wore his WWI uniform with celluloid collars which he 'cleaned' with an eraser! For shaving, his razor blades were sharpened on glass. His 'waste not, want not' attitude was likewise passed on to colleagues. Thus, anyone requesting a pencil would be likely to receive a stub. Moreover, if you requested a pin, that is all you would receive - one pin![7]

A further example of an unusual character is a PO who had the misfortune to be cross-eyed. This caused amusement, and confusion, among the ranks on parade at times. He would stand in front of an apprentice and yell 'Get your **** hair cut!' The apprentice concerned might reply that he had, in fact, already had his hair cut to which the PO would respond that he wasn't talking to him, but to the next in line![8]

In complete contrast to these characters, there were the more mature officers who, whilst demanding high standards, were very much respected. In addition to their normal Instructors' responsibilities, a number assisted in organising sporting events and various forms of entertainment. This included dances and variety shows using talented members from all branches of the armed services locally. These events were also for the benefit of the general public and often were in aid of local charities.[9]

NOTES

1. John White. Letter to author 25th April 1996
2. Fred Lovell. op.cit
3. Ron Harper. op.cit
4. The author is grateful to John White for this information
5. Alf Richardson. Interview with author 18th September 1996
6. Alf Richardson. Interview with author 6th November 1996
7. Fred Lovell. op.cit
8. Dave Lane. Letter to author 15th January 1998
9. Ken Gavin. Letter to author 22nd February 1997

1st Benbow Division Apprentices after Passing Out, June 1942, HMS Daedalus II. Clayton Hall.

Courtesy J Carnill

1st Grenville Division Apprentices at Clayton Hall, 1942.

Courtesy L Bear

Chapter Nine
THE SOCIAL SCENE

Surprisingly perhaps, the social life of North Staffordshire during World War II was described as 'pretty hectic'. Newcastle-under-Lyme alone boasted four cinemas, together with several venues where dances were held regularly, including the Municipal Hall and the Castle Hotel. Coupled with this there were vast numbers of female workers in the area, employed in munitions and other factories, and living away from home. Furthermore, the ranks of service personnel already based locally were always swollen by those on leave. Many, including former personnel from Daedalus II, can recall being caught up in the atmosphere, having fond memories of the dances at the Municipal Hall. Some of these were organised by the Borough Council, and at the end of the war, tributes were paid to the work of the Services Entertainments Committee.[1]

Mrs Sylvia King recalls that the young Daedalus apprentices had little or no money and girls tended to pay for themselves on such occasions. However, they were only admitted to the 'Muni' dances accompanied by someone in uniform. Consequently, unaccompanied girls initially 'paraded' outside the building, or waited on the main steps. Every so often a doorman let a few in, otherwise apprentices arriving in uniform would be accosted to take a girl into the dance, but almost always paying for themselves.[2] Some apprentices operated a ruse at the Saturday night dances. According to Mrs S. Ridgeway, having gained entry to the function, some would obtain a pass to come out. They would then return to regain entry with a waiting girl. However, perhaps being unaware that he had already been into the premises, she would give him the price of entry for the two! Then, having shown his pass and paid for the girl, the surplus cash would be pocketed and this might be accomplished on a number of occasions during the evening.[3]

Having left school, Sylvia King was employed at the North Staffs Laundry in Basford. Here, by an arrangement with the Admiralty, all the apprentices's washing was regularly attended to on the premises. Sylvia recollects that notes were sometimes included in the bundles of laundry requesting blind dates. After consulting colleagues, it was sometimes learned that the writer might be unpopular for some reason. If this were the case, it was not unknown for the girls to remove the cord from his pyjamas, or worse still, starch his shirt tails![4]

Other popular venues for dances included Lewis's, Hanley, and the King's Hall in Stoke-on-Trent, but they were also held on occasion in the newly built gymnasium at Clayton Hall, particularly for passing out celebrations. When the Americans entered the war, they too organised dances at Crewe Hall and Stone, and Wrens from Daedalus II were always invited to attend. Transport was provided by the Americans and these vehicles were known as 'liberty buses' or 'passion wagons!'[5]

Cinemas were a popular source of entertainment, particularly in Newcastle-under-Lyme. Here again, a highly successful although dishonest enterprise was in operation by the apprentices. Admission to two of the town's cinemas was obtained by the purchase of a metal tally, instead of the customary ticket. Before long, a metal tally production line was in operation via the lathes of the Blackfriars workshops, providing apprentices with free admission facilities! Ron Watt (Effingham Division) also revealed that a few of the more daring apprentices used to slip out of class at the workshops to take in the occasional afternoon film at a nearby cinema. This was achieved by proceeding to the toilet, shedding one's overalls and leaving the building by climbing through a window. Then, by crossing an area of waste land, access to the cinema could by gained through the rear door. After the performance, the apprentice would return by the same route, emerge whistling from the toilet and innocently make his way back to his lathe! Ron could not recall anyone getting caught.[6]

Wrestling was yet another popular form of entertainment during the period, and Daedalus personnel were among the regular attenders at the events held at Hanley's Victoria Hall. However, at times, John Williams (2nd Grenville Division) and some of his colleagues were shocked at the behaviour of certain members of the audience. Apparently, it was not unusual for some of the ladies to be seen 'belting some of the wrestlers with their handbags as they left the ring'. On other occasions, 'bottles were thrown during bouts!'[7]

For the more culturally inclined, there were regular concerts at the same venue, particularly by the Halle Orchestra under the baton of Sir John Barbirolli, and the Royal Liverpool Philarmonic conducted by Dr (later Sir) Malcolm Sargeant. Attending with friends and colleagues gave some service personnel the chance to hear classical music for the first time which they learnt to appreciate. Also, some Daedalus II personnel, particularly Wrens, took an opportunity to join the newly formed Ceramic City Choir and performed at the premises. There was no shortage of first class artistes appearing at the Victoria Hall, and during the war period these included the likes of Joan Hammond (soprano), Heddle Nash (tenor), Gladys Riply (contralto), Kathleen Ferrier (contralto), Leon Goossens (oboe) and pianist Moiseiwitsch. According to former Wren 2nd Officer Victoria Erskine, 'her happiest times at Newcastle were attending the most wonderful concerts at the Victoria Hall'. Favourite soloists that she heard locally included Kathleen Ferrier and the pianist Solomon.[8] There is little doubt that an evening of good music was not to be missed as far as North Staffs audiences were concerned. The Victoria Hall was always packed on such occasions and the performances were regarded as a good antidote to raise depressed spirits through the dark years of the war. They provided a form of escapism and, according to Angus Calder, thousands were attracted to music for the first time.[9]

The venue also played host to the great jazz stars of the era. Ray Kennedy (1st Grenville Division) recalls 'breaking ship' to see trumpeter Nat Gonella. Unfortunately, having made his way to Hanley, he was unable to obtain a ticket and so, after a visit to the YMCA, he walked back to Clayton Hall. To his dismay, whilst in the process of scrambling over the establishment's security fence, he was spotted by a 'bad tempered' PO. He and a sentry gave chase but Ray managed to reach his hut whereupon he jumped into bed, fully clothed and still wearing his boots! Moments later when the Duty Officer and staff entered the room, Ray was feigning sleep. They were heard to say 'well, he's in' and, on that occasion, Ray was fortunate in escaping retribution.[10]

Although forbidden by the Navy to drink or smoke under the age of 18 years, apprentices did nevertheless frequent local pubs, particularly relishing the cider which was 6d per pint. Favourite hostelries recalled include The Compasses (now The Crossways), The Victoria, and The Bird in Hand (now The Farrow & Firkin). The Boat & Horses and The Sutherland Arms were not so popular with British servicemen after American troops began to use them on a regular basis. On licensed premises, apprentices had to be always on the alert because of Navy Police patrols which often appeared unannounced. However, if this occurred at The Victoria, the publican hid apprentices temporarily in the cellar.[11]

Times being what they were, the personnel of HMS Daedalus II were multi-talented. Many were instrumentalists to a standard that ensured them a place in the unit band or dance band. Consequently, they were capable of providing their own entertainment, and did not have to rely on that provided for them. Various events were organised by the officers, including CPO Tim Gavin. Keen to enrich the social life of the base, Gavin not only organised shows at Clayton Hall, but also at the town's Municipal Hall using talented members from all branches of the services. His daughter Alice, a semi-professional dancer, regularly performed solos at these events, her speciality being a dual tap/ballet routine in which she tap danced on her toes. Tim's son, Ken, recalls their house in Audley Place reverberating with the sound of practising musicians, some of whom became professionals.[12] Another popular act recalled is that of Abbott & Hale. John Abbott and John Hale (2nd Benbow Division) impersonated the famous Western Brothers at Christmas concerts and parties.[13] For those unfamiliar with the name, Kenneth and George Western were a popular radio and variety act. They always wore tails and monocles (similar to Ray Charles' ventriloquist dummy 'Lord Charles') and, according to Roy Hudd, played the characters of 'two silly arses.' Their laconic, laid back 'remember the old school tie' and 'play the game you cads' delivery belied their topical and very often sharp, satirical monologues to music. The Western Brothers were masters at 'sending up' the establishment and, in some ways. were ahead of their time.[14]

'Home' entertainment was also provided by those fortunate enough to have a gramophone and records. Ray Kennedy had a few jazz records including Glenn Miller's 'Sunrise Serenade' and Artie Shaw's 'Begin the Beguine' with which he entertained his colleagues, sometimes himself 'swinging away playing an imaginery clarinet to the music'.[15] Others, such as Jack Carnill (1st Benbow Division) organised a music club utilising the unit's gramophone in the recreation room of Clayton Hall.[16]

Other popular social occasions were the parties held at the Wrennery to which locals would also be invited. In recalling the events, Malcolm Williams remembers the premises being 'festooned with bunting' and having 'a wonderful atmosphere'.[17] Former Wren 2nd Officer Victoria Erskine confirms that they had some very good parties in the WRNS quarters. She believed that the best were at Halloween.[18]

Trentham Gardens was a favourite haunt with the majority of service personnel. Essentially, this was because of the 'abundance of talent' to quote various sources. Of particular interest for the fair sex were large numbers of French servicemen who were encamped in Trentham Park in 1940, subsequently followed by an officer cadet training unit and an extensive service convalescent unit. For the males, the staff of the London Clearing Banks were present in the ballroom, the majority of whom were female. In addition, there was frequent entertainment in the form of shows and dances.

Former Wren Pat Welsh (now Mrs Prosser) attended a six month Air Mechanics (L) course at HMS Daedalus II in 1942. She and her colleagues would hire a boat, row into the middle of Trentham Lake and 'cast aside the oars deliberately, in order that some gallant male(s) would come to their rescue!' She also recalls the frequent practice of Daedalus apprentices hiring a boat for two persons, and then picking up friends or colleagues further down the lake. Pat thoroughly enjoyed her time in North Staffordshire, in particular dancing and parties at the Castle Hotel.[19] Alf Richardson (Effingham Division) also recollects occasions when he and his colleagues gained free admission to the Trentham swimming baths. It was policy to charge admission for individuals, but parties from service establishments such as Daedalus were admitted free of charge. Consequently, a number of apprentices would meet at the Trentham Gardens entrance, tuck their towels, etc under their arms, form up into a squad and march in unchallenged![20]

Obviously, 'talent spotting' was not confined to Trentham or North Staffordshire in general. It went on almost anywhere and at any time and some service personnel perfected this to a fine art. Sunday evenings in Newcastle were known as 'town walking nights' and were regarded as good occasions to seek out members of the opposite sex on the 'monkey run.' According to Sylvia King, girls would sometimes just stand and talk to the apprentices, some would go for a walk, whilst others would pair off'.[21] Of course this practice was not unique to apprentices. Thanks to the precarious wartime situation, people had affairs, fell in love, or did outrageous things as if there was no tomorrow because, for some, unfortunately there wasn't! Otherwise romances lasted a week, perhaps a month or even longer, but several local girls did marry personnel from HMS Daedalus II. Thankfully, they remain happily married today.

Apprentices relaxing in NAAFI Canteen. Daedalus II, Clayton.

Courtesy J Fowler

NOTES

1. NBC. Minutes of Council 30th October 1945.
2. Mrs Sylia King. Interview with author June 1997
3. Mrs S. Ridgeway. Interview with author 22nd April 1996
4. Mrs Sylvia King op.cit
5. Mrs Kathleen Barton op.cit
6. Ron Watt. Letter to author November 1997
7. John Williams. Telephone call to author 23rd July 1997
8. Miss Victoria Erskine. Letter to author 10th June 1997
9. Angus Calder The People's War (Pimlico) p373
10. Ray Kennedy op.cit
11. Alf Richardson op.cit
12. Ken Gavin op.cit
13. John White. Unpublished ode - 'Hale & hearty' (Oct 1994) - author's collection
14. Roy Hudd. Cavalcade of Variety Acts (Robson Books) p193
15. Ray Kennedy op.cit
16. Jack Carnill. Interview with author 14th September 1996
17. Malcolm Williams op.cit
18. Miss Victoria Erskine op.cit
19. Mrs Pat Prosser. Interview with author 19th September 1996
20. Alf Richardson. Interview with author 18th September 1996
21. Mrs Sylvia King op.cit

Chapter Ten
YANKS AND BEVIN BOYS

During the early period of World War II, the Fleet Air Arm made a great impact on Newcastle-under-Lyme, not least its social life. They were very popular with the girls and very much had the field to themselves. However, the subsequent arrival locally of American forces making their belated entrance into the war, then the Bevin boys, gave rise to rivalries which sometimes exploded into physical violence on a significant scale.

The first American troops arrived in the United Kingdom in early 1942. By May 1944 there were 1½ million US soldiers, sailors and airmen stationed here, poised to assist in the launch of an allied offensive on Hitler's 'Fortress Europe'. It was a colossal build up. Americans seemed to be everywhere. Convoys of transport whined through the blacked out streets, and the country's dance halls and pubs seemed to be full of American uniforms. The nearest American camps to Newcastle-under-Lyme were Keele Hall, Crewe Hall and Nelson Hall, near Cotes Heath.

Most British people had never encountered real live Americans before the arrival of the US troops. As Juliet Gardiner observed - 'their image had been shaped by weekly visits to the cinema where America was depicted as a load of chromium plated sophistication and wealth, if it wasn't the Wild West!'[1]

The average weekly pay of US privates and corporals was nearly five times that of their British counterparts. This was largely spent on girls, drink, cigarettes and entertainment. In addition to this, they could purchase goods at their PXs (equivalent of NAAFIs) at subsidised prices, including food, most of which was shipped from the United States. Apart from the financial aspect, other factors proved to be an attraction to some of the British girls. The American troops used deodorants and aftershave, cosmetic items completely unknown to British men at the time. It seemed, too, that they had access to an endless supply of nylons! Also, former World War II British servicemen concede that the Americans 'outclassed' them in appearance, as the US uniforms were of a far superior quality.[2] Whilst this may be so, locals nevertheless maintain that when both American and British troops were on parade together at Newcastle, the British outshone the Americans as far as bearing and drill was concerned.

To the young men of Britain, whether in uniform or otherwise, the American troops were seen as a threat, and when tensions flared up between the two, the disagreements were generally about girls, or perhaps due to too much alcohol. Much drunkenness was reported among the American troops, particularly in the Manchester and Liverpool areas and it was not unknown for them to drink a pub dry.[3] Misunderstandings also arose, on occasion, merely as a result of differences in the meaning of language!

Ken Gavin recalls one particular incident at The Talbot (now The Shalimar) in Church Street, Newcastle in which a 'quite large' American soldier, seemingly unhappy with the progress that a Fleet Air Arm member was making with some girls, chose to pick a fight. As it happened, the latter was an accomplished boxer who, having knocked the American to the ground, added to his indignity by dragging and dumping him outside, before moving on elsewhere. His pride hurt, the American returned with some colleagues who savagely beat up another young member of the Fleet Air Arm who knew nothing of the earlier incident. His resultant injuries were such that he was hospitalised for quite a time. According to Ken, news spread quickly and the next night, to a man, the Fleet Air Arm went to sort out the Americans at one of their favourite watering holes, The Smithfield public house. The resultant battle spilled over from the pub up into the town centre where the two sides fought with bricks, bottles and just about everything which came to hand. Peace was only restored with the arrival on the scene of both American and Royal Navy military police patrols who jointly brought the situation under control.[4] Former Wren PO Joyce Butcher (now Mrs Richardson) also recalls one morning in 1943 when there was a 'buzz' going around about an incident at The Talbot on the previous evening. On that particular morning, a number of male colleagues, who like her were on an Air Mechanic Electrician's course, arrived in the classroom with 'black eyes, hands bandaged and looking a somewhat woeful lot!' It transpired that they had been involved in a fracas with a number of Mexicans from a local American unit. After this, The Talbot was declared out of bounds for a period.[5]

On another occasion, a number of drunken Americans on leaving The Sutherland Arms assaulted the lone guard on duty outside Daedalus's Smithfield Workshops. This, according to Mrs S. Ridgeway, almost resulted in war between the two factions and, for a time, American troops were barred from the town. She also recalls an incident at one of the Municipal Hall functions when a large American serviceman was dancing with his girlfriend. Uninfluenced by this, one of the young Daedalus apprentices attempted to cut in. Taking exception, the American took off his jacket preparing to fight, little realising that the apprentice was a martial arts exponent. The resultant bout put the American on the floor three times! As a consequence, a rumour soon spread that all the apprentices undertook martial arts training and, for a while at least, tension between the two factions eased.[6]

The Fleet Air Arm was to experience further rivalry for the local girls with the arrival of the Bevin Boys. Named after Ernest Bevin, the then Minister of Labour, the Bevin Boy scheme resulted in one out of every ten young males available for the armed services being conscripted into the mines. By its introduction, the Government acknowledged the importance of the coal mining industry at a most crucial stage of World War II, and over 20,000 were diverted to fulfill this role.[7] Like the Americans, they too were more affluent than the naval apprentices. Those in the Newcastle-under-Lyme area lived in billets or at a hostel in Knutton.

It is acknowledged that some Bevin Boys were difficult to handle. Generally, they regarded the mining occupation as 'degrading' and 'were determined that everyone should know that they did not accept their enforced entry into the mines willingly or with good grace.' According to David Day, in such cases, 'their attitude towards their instructors and other pit officials was deliberately provocative'.[8] This attitude was not conducive to a happy situation, in any event.

A number of former Daedalus apprentices referred to constant fighting with Bevin Boys. Jack Carnill (1st Benbow Division) recollects that one morning, following a particularly serious incident in Hanley involving Daedalus personnel, the Commanding Officer told those on morning parade that 'such behaviour will not be tolerated' but added 'you handled the situation very well!'[9] Mr F.A. Peters (1st Grenville Division) also recalls frequent occurrences of some of the youngest apprentices being 'badly molested' and 'physically injured' by Bevin Boys as they returned to Daedalus at night. Despite protests from the naval authorities to the civil police, they seemed unwilling or unable to prevent the incidents. Consequently, according to my correspondent, the apprentices held a series of meetings with a view to resolving the situation. News of this reached the ears of the Executive Commander and on the Saturday morning he called a special parade. Indicating that he knew what they had in mind, he went on to say that he hoped that they would 'behave like gentlemen and not use any weapons like knuckle dusters!' Finally he added that only the minimum number of personnel would be required for duty. His words resulted in a mass exodus and later that evening the 'rogue Bevin Boys were waylaid by devious means!' Having suffered just punishment, their reign of terror was brought to an end - at least temporarily.[10]

With the presence of the various services, military and/or naval patrols were familiar sights in the town, particularly at night. Often in the charge of a CPO or PO, the naval patrols generally consisted of six or so ratings who would proceed in file, two abreast with a peculiar gait, in the road, approximately 1ft from the kerb. According to Ken Gavin, their presence was usually enough to bring out the best behaviour in naval personnel, but local youths sometimes considered that they were fair game for taunting, believing themselves to be safe from reprisal. However, Ken's father, a CPO who himself had represented the Royal Navy as a boxer, had other ideas! On at least one occasion, Ken recalls, his father allowed one of his patrol, usually an enthusiastic young boxer, to take on one of the tormentors at the rear of the town's Masonic Lodge. As Ken says - 'end of problem!'[11]

NOTES

1. Juliet Gardiner. Over Here - the GI's in Wartime Britain (Collis & Brown) p111
2. Ibid p113
3. Ibid p80
4. Ken Gavin op.cit
5. Mrs Joyce Richardson. Letter to author 14th February 1998
6. Mrs S. Ridgeway op.cit
7. David Day. The Bevin Boy (Ashford, Buchan & Enright, Leatherhead) p2
8. Ibid p16
9. Jack Carnill. Interview with author 30th October 1996
10. Mr F.A. Peters. Letter to author 6th April 1997
11. Ken Gavin op.cit

Members of the 1st Grenville Division relaxing to records, HMS Daedalus, Clayton, 1940

Courtesy R Kennedy

Former YMCA premises, Higherland Chapel, Newcastle, where many Daedalus apprentices enjoyed meal breaks.

Courtesy F King

1st Grenville Division taken at Clayton, 1942, with Commander Gifford, Captain Moore and Lieutenant Dibben (centre front).

Courtesy F King

The contents of one wooden hut - all members 2nd Grenville Division, HMS Daedalus, Clayton Hall, 1944. John Williams, who supplied the photograph, is third from the left on the front row. CPO Apprentice A R King, who was in charge of the hut, is next to him. (See chevrons on sleeves).

Three personnel from HMS Daedalus II out on the town and about to sample the brew at the former Bird in Hand public house, Hassell Street, Newcastle.
Courtesy Ron Harper

Fleet Air Arm. Grenville Division.

Apprentices

request the pleasure of your company at their

Passing Out Party

In the Royal Venetian Chamber, Holborn Restaurant,

On Friday, December 18th, 1942.

Anchors aweigh 6-15 p.m. Don't be adrift!

Cabaret. Dancing. Refreshments.

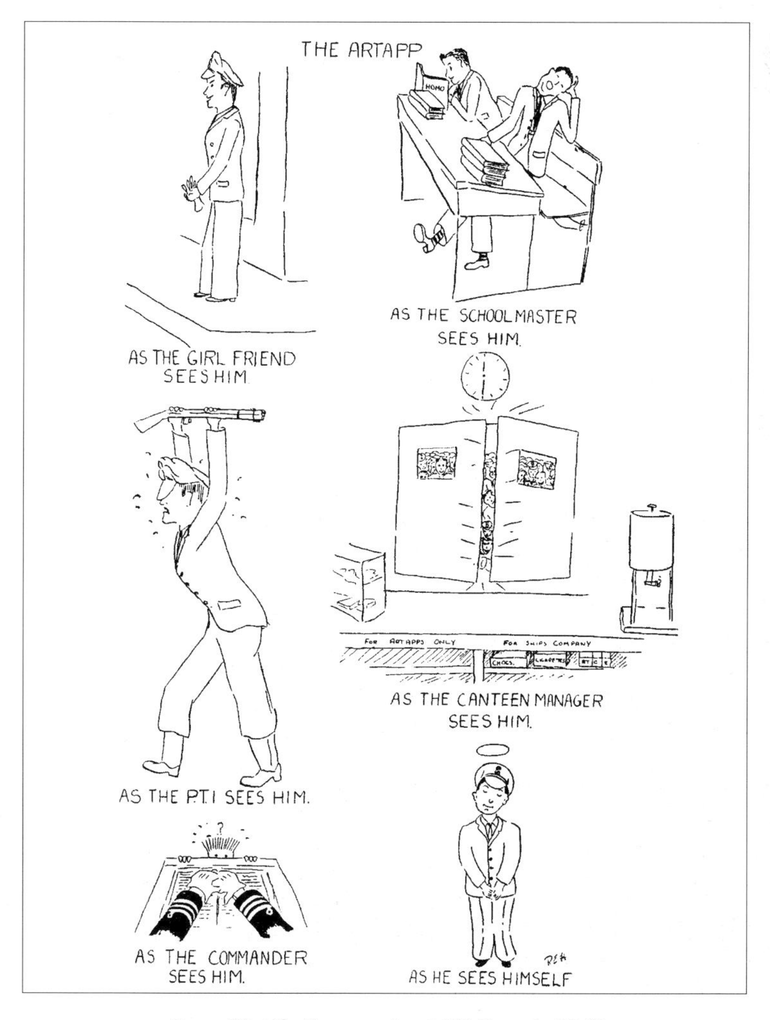

From "Artifex" magazine MTE Rosyth 1942.

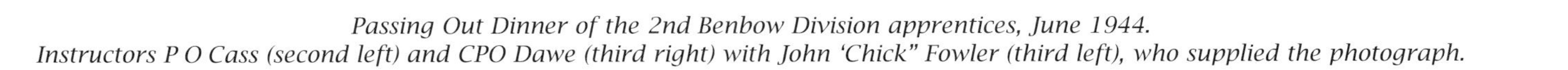

Passing Out Dinner of the 2nd Benbow Division apprentices, June 1944.
Instructors P O Cass (second left) and CPO Dawe (third right) with John 'Chick" Fowler (third left), who supplied the photograph.

Chapter Eleven
THE GRAPES OF ROTHWELL

When pushed to the limit, everyone has a physical or mental breaking point. It is simply a question of how much an individual can take, but to go beyond this limit can lead to some form of protest. In the armed forces, such action could be classed as mutiny, depending on the scale or form of retaliatory action.

Food, or the standard of it, was a major bone of contention at Clayton Hall, particularly in the early to mid part of the war. As a consequence there were, on occasion, protests or acts of defiance by Daedalus apprentices, but whether any of these occurrences were classed as mutiny is now difficult to determine. I gather, however, it is more likely that a veil may have been drawn over some, if not all, of the incidents.

With all the physical activity, the apprentices were always hungry, and they would supplement their intake of food in any way possible. Some would even walk to the Stoke railway station canteen where a cup of tea and a bun could always be obtained free of charge. Others welcomed food parcels from home, or accepted meals at the homes of girlfriends where they were welcomed, despite rationing and a shortage of food generally. One popular additional source of nourishment was to be found in the form of unrationed miniature malt loaves which were available from Greenhalgh's store in Northwood Lane, Clayton. When apprentices were marching to the hangars there, one would slip out of the column to purchase a number of loaves which would be shared out later at 'stand easy'.[1] Similarly, malt loaves could be purchased from a small baker's premises on Clayton Bank by those apprentices who were attending classes in the town.[2] Otherwise, for those fortunate enough to possess a little pocket money, good cheap snacks were always available from the YMCA hut at Higherland. For 2½d, a cup of tea and a rock cake could be bought or alternatively, beans on toast, or a slice of toast spread with jam priced 1d.[3]

A prime example of the standard of food served at Clayton Hall is illustrated by an incident recalled from the early war period. Fred King (1st Grenville Division) acknowledges that the food was 'not too clever at times', but he particularly remembers an occasion when green meat was served up. This resulted in complaints to the Officer of the Day who ate a sample. However, having commented that 'it was all right', he hurried outside where he was 'violently sick!'[4]

Rissoles were extremely unpopular with the apprentices. Manufactured from 'spuds and pilchards', descriptions of the finished product vary from 'awful' to 'horrible' (and even worse!). Thus, perhaps not surprisingly, in one incident when the Officer of the Day refused to act on complaints, the offending rissoles were 'thrown at the galley'.[5] On another occasion, untouched portions were heaped onto plates and returned to the servery with forks pushed in! This resulted in an altercation with a 'stroppy' Wren, and having been charged with swearing at her, one apprentice received 'twelve cuts' (ie birching).[6] Ray Kennedy (1st Grenville Division) confirms that apprentices had to be 'nice' to the Wrens in the galley, otherwise one might be on a charge or, worse still, receive no 'afters'![7]

Eddie Cuthbert (2nd Benbow Division) remembers one particular night when a few adventurous colleagues returned to their hut bearing one of the Captain's chickens, having raided their enclosure. He told the writer that 'no doubt young growing teenagers being forever hungry inspired the theft.' First, it was agreed that the feathers were easily disposable and could be burnt in the hut stove. As to the actual cooking, it was decided to encase the carcass in clay and place it in the stove. However, one problem became immediately evident. Having encased the bird in clay, it was too large to insert into the aperture of the stove. To solve the problem, dissection of the chicken into smaller pieces was decided upon, a solution achieved with the aid of a 'not very sharp' penknife. 'The chicken was literally hacked to pieces', he recalled. Again, it was packed in clay and placed on hot coke in the stove. However, removal of the finished product presented yet a further problem due to limited access to the stove, and burns were experienced in the attempt! This also resulted in 'billowing clouds of smoke from the burning chicken pieces pervading the hut' and it 'obviously stank the place out!' It was then realised that they had failed to notice the time. The Officer of the Day was due in 30 minutes on his 9 o'clock round, when the huts were due to be inspected for tidiness, cleaniness and good naval order. Those involved felt sure that he would not fail to identify the smell of cooked poultry, and that this in turn would be linked with the Captain's missing chicken. As a consequence, every door and window was flung open to relieve the smell and then one occupant of the hut had 'a touch of genius!' What about burning a gym shoe to disguise the aroma? One was hastily pushed into the stove. The Officer of the Day duly appeared, commented on the awful smell but, thankfully, continued on his rounds! No further action was taken on this occasion.[8] Interestingly, from time to time attempts were also made to procure chickens from neighbouring farms, with the aid of a hockey stick!

By far the most serious protest occurred in 1944 with the so called 'Grapes of Rothwell' incident. The story in itself has developed something of a legendary quality over the years and has been recounted on numerous occasions at reunions. Lt. Commander (E) C. Rothwell, the ship's Executive Commander, made extensive use of the greenhouses at Clayton Hall, particularly the vines. Having found that some of his grapes were missing, he ordered all leave to be stopped until the culprits were found. As a result, the apprentices marched in protest to the quarterdeck, tore down the flag from the mast and hoisted a red jersey! Hearing the disturbance, the Officer of the Day came out of the Hall to investigate, but hastily beat a retreat back inside the building. Several then marched on the guardroom where the RPOs locked themselves in, whilst other apprentices went into town where, as John Williams observed, 'a number of them already had their feet under the table!' Armed local units were immediately brought in to surround the Hall complex and to contain the situation as it was feared that a more serious confrontation might arise. The apprentices, after all, had access to guns and ammunition. Thankfully, peace was restored after the culprits confessed and the necessary evidence, in the form of seeds, found. Gradually, life at the establishment returned to normal. In the meantime, several of the apprentices secretly left the site and made their way into town to assist those of their colleagues to return via unguarded check points. It was eventually established that two had gone overboard (ie deserted) and they were subsequently dismissed the service.[9]

NOTES

1. John White. Letter to author 16th April 1996
2. Ron Watt op.cit
3. Dave Lane op.cit
4. Fred King. Interview with author 12th November 1996
5. Alf Richardson op.cit
6. John Williams op.cit
7. Ray Kennedy op.cit
8. F.E. Cuthbert. Letter to author 27th April 1996
9. John Williams op.cit

Chapter Twelve
THE SECOND GUNPOWDER PLOT

Use of explosives, ballistics, bombs and other armaments formed part of the in-depth training of ordnance apprentices. Eddie Cuthbert (2nd Benbow Division) remembers receiving instruction on the wondrous workings of a 3" maroon mortar which had a friction operated initiator for the gunpowder sack that propelled the maroon projectile several hundred feet into the air. He recalls this particularly because in the course of the live demonstration, 'a number of the propellant bags of gunpowder went missing!' Subsequently, a group of the apprentices using some of their newly acquired knowledge carried out experiments in secret with explosives in various odd containers using differing levels of charges and designer type fuses. 'We got the hang of it' he commented, 'just about the time our instructor NCOs decided to have a party in their mess.' 'Some of these had given us a bad time' he continued, 'and no doubt we were very envious of their privileges, so the second gunpowder plot was hatched!'

The NCOs' facility was located in a Nissen type building in the grounds of Clayton Hall and on the evening of the event, a careful approach was made using shrubbery and darkness for cover. At an opportune moment the device was fused and inserted into the aperture between the corrugated tin forming the outer wall of the building and the inner skin. The perpetrators then retired to view the effect of the explosion. They did not have to wait long! The device exploded and, as part of the design included smoke generator filling, a suitably effective smoke cloud resulted. The device was small and not designed to cause a big explosion. On the contrary, the main element was smoke. After a short while the hut spewed forth very irate NCOs with their wives and girlfriends and, at this point, the miscreants fled! Apparently there was an inquiry later, but no persons were charged with any offences. Whilst no one was hurt during the incident, Eddie now acknowledges that 'with hindsight, it was a stupid thing to do. But it was typical of pranks that prevailed at the time'.[1] Another trick making use of newly acquired knowledge involved electrifying door handles for the benefit of CPOs and NCOs!

A less scientific approach was used in the case of pranks relating to canteen tea urns. Personnel would help themselves to mugs of tea from these large vessels at mealtimes. On occasion, salt, pepper, and/or mustard would be discreetly poured into the urns, and then given a good shake to mix up the brew. It was then a question of waiting to see who would get caught trying to drink the concoction![2]

Other antics included the practice of performing dares which sometimes would be for payment of cash. A prime example involved attempting to sit on the top of a hut stove for a stated period. Once the conditions had been agreed, the apparatus was stoked up until it was white hot, and it was on such an occasion that the late Harry Adams (2nd Benbow Division) accepted a challenge to sit on the stove for 3 seconds. Several times he jumped clear, just short of the time. Yet a further dare to sit on the stove for one second was successfully attempted. But he was in extreme pain, not surprisingly, having lost an amount of skin from his buttocks. It so happens that Harry was Divisional Bugler which necessitated cycling around the Clayton Hall complex. It is difficult to imagine how he performed this task whilst his self inflicted wounds healed![3]

Another prank related to those poor unfortunates who were on 8A punishment. Sometimes, offenders would purposely drink too much 'kai' (cocoa made with thick blocks of a kind of chocolate) before running/doubling in full kit (known as the '8A shuffle'), or 'crow hopping' with a rifle. The intention of this was to become sick and thus, hopefully, be able to skive off. However, some officers and NCOs became aware of the practice, and any offender caught might be placed in the position where he had to suffer even more punishment.[4]

Inter-divisional 'battles' were fought at times. Favourite 'weapons' included knotted towels with a lump of soap in the knot, and airborne canvas slippers. Raids were also made on the junior division dormitories by members of the senior divisions. Sometimes, a junior 'hostage' would be captured and taken back to one of the senior dormitories where he might be forced to push a pea or a 6d piece along the floor with his nose, or perhaps perform some other humiliating task. In the winter period, it was also not unknown for senior apprentices to drop snowballs down the chimneys of junior division huts and then, at a given signal, rush in and overturn the beds!

When 'going ashore', and as soon as they were clear of the main gate on Clayton Road, the majority of off-duty apprentices would take off their caps and remove the metal grommet. (The inserted grommet was necessary to pass inspection). The cap would then be replaced on the head, perhaps at a jaunty angle, and smoothed down to each individual's taste. A little further along the road, a number usually turned right into Clayton Lane where they would strip off their rough serge single breasted uniforms. On the other side of the hedge the duty sentry would be waiting to fulfill his role as a sort of cloakroom attendant, the trees behind him being festooned with uniforms on hangers, diagonal serge and doeskin, all double breasted. In turn, these were handed over, the sentry taking in the discarded uniforms to be collected later. Soon, a bunch of much smarter apprentices were on their way to town! It was also not unusual for some apprentices to return to Clayton Hall looking much slimmer than when they went 'ashore'. This was because earlier, they had been wearing extra shirts, pyjamas, pullovers, etc which they sold in the pubs in town![5]

The antics of the apprentices quoted are merely a few examples of what prevailed at the time. Some of the pranks were phenomenal, even legendary and, to everyone's delight, continue to be a source of amusement today at reunions.

NOTES
1. F.E. Cuthbert op.cit
2. John White op.cit
3. Ibid
4. John Williams op.cit
5. Ron Watt op.cit

Chapter Thirteen
THE FLEDGLINGS

On 15th April 1943 a 'sister' establishment to HMS Daedalus II was commissioned at Mill Meece, a few miles south of Clayton. Situated in the beautiful undulating North Staffordshire countryside, HMS Fledgling also came under the control of HMS Daedalus I at Lee-on-Solent. Despite its brief life, HMS Fledgling has a number of claims to fame, yet sadly it seems to have been largely forgotten. It was the *first* purely WRNS technical training establishment. Secondly, it was then the only naval air station fully manned by the Royal Navy, although there were one or two instructors who had transferred from the RAF to the Fleet Air Arm.[1] In addition, as the war progressed, HMS Fledgling was to train personnel from overseas. Consequently, its role in the war effort should not be underestimated.

Fledgling was located to the rear of the infamous Royal Ordnance Factory, Swynnerton, not perhaps the most ideal of situations! ROF 55 Swynnerton was a 'filling factory', in other words shell, bomb and land mine cases, together with fuses and high explosives such as TNT, were transported here from other factories for assembly into the finished product. Not surprisingly, it was a site much sought after by the Luftwaffe on its nightly bombing raids and there are those to this day who firmly believe that it was saved as a result of the frequent mists which shroud the Meece Valley, thus hiding it from the eyes of enemy air crews. Radar, of course, was not available in aircraft at the time. Fledgling's staff and trainees were housed in accommodation released by the Ministry of Supply and which had been formerly utilised by those who had been employed on building the ROF.

Fledgling's Commanding Officer was Captain Percy R.P. Percival. Promoted to Midshipman in 1903, Percival had risen steadily through the ranks to achieve a distinguished naval career. He had seen plenty of action during World War I and had been awarded the DSO for action against German destroyers off the Belgian coast on 21st March 1918. After the war he continued in command of destroyers, retiring from the service in 1932. Like many of his contemporaries, he was recalled to the colours in 1939 at the outbreak of World War II.[2] Percival and his famous Old English Sheepdog were familiar sights at the station and in the locality, and a few local residents remember them fondly to this day. He remained in charge of HMS Fledgling until it closed at the end of the war.

According to a contemporary report, much was accomplished in a short time by the ship's company to achieve satisfactory adaptation of the buildings, etc to Admiralty requirements. Some of the work was undertaken by maintenance staff from HMS Daedalus II under Shipwright Lt. S.C. McClounan. PO Joiner Frank Plant can recall working at Fledgling where, at times, he was the only man! Having 'caught a packet' from a German Stuka during the seige of Tobruk, Frank had spent some time recuperating from his injuries before being posted to Daedalus II. Thankfully, he admitted it was 'much quieter' at Mill Meece than Tobruk, and the Fledgling girls 'spoiled him at times!'[3]

As in the case of HMS Daedalus II, Fledgling's training schemes provided for the four categories of Air Mechanics - Airframe (A), Engine (E), Electrician (L), and Ordnance (or armament) (O). In addition, all trainees attended classes for extra and applied maths, and also given lectures on such subjects as the history of flying, types of aircraft in use by the Fleet Air Arm and the duties of a naval air station. There were about 40 instructors employed at Mill Meece, mainly CPOs and POs, and these were under the control of Lt.

Wrens of Class 01, HMS Fledgling, under the instruction of CPO Worsley at the Armoury of HMS Daedalus, Newcastle-under-Lyme. August 1943.

Courtesy Mrs Pam Lawler

Wrens learning about the intricacies of the Barracuda engine, HMS Fledgling, 1944.

Courtesy Helen Proctor

Cdr (E) W.E.Budge. Some of the instructors came in as required from Daedalus II. Also, Ordnance Mechanics received some training there until the Mill Meece workshops were fully equipped.

Nevertheless, the station had an array of equipment for training purposes from the beginning, and extensive use was also made of modern teaching aids such as educational films. The Air Mechanics (E) had the benefit of having access to an abundance of engines for training purposes which could be stripped and reassembled as necessary. Also, Ordnance Mechanics had the benefit of being able to work on examples of every aircraft gun in service with the Fleet Air Arm. They were taught how to strip the guns, clean and reassemble them. They also studied details of different types of ammunition and recoil systems, and learned just about everything that could go wrong and how to carry out repairs swiftly and efficiently. There was also a ''bomb alley' containing examples of models of all types of bombs in use on naval aircraft. In addition, the station had a small fleet of aircraft for ground handling and other practice. Amongst others, these included a Corsair, a Wildcat, a Fulmar, a Blackburn Shark, a Hurricane and a Percival Proctor.[4]

Courses for all categories lasted about 18 weeks, with examinations every 4 weeks. Class sizes were about 15 trainees, and for practical work there were 2 instructors per class. HMS Fledgling was commissioned to produce a steady stream of well trained Wren Air Mechanics, the intention being to save manpower in the hardpressed Royal Navy. At the time, it was estimated that resultant savings would be in the region of 25%-30%.[5]

Most of the girls found the area around the station to be very pleasant, sentiments which they have retained over the years. Waxing lyrical, one described it as 'farming country, gently undulating with a lot of trees, little streams and dozens of intersecting lanes which were very pleasant for cycling'.[6] What they didn't find so desirable was the close proximity of the Royal Ordnance Factory. For example, one correspondent recalls attending open air services at HMS Fledgling when the area of the parade ground (or quarterdeck) would suddenly become thick with smoke from the ROF as testing of ammunition commenced.[7] Another formed the opinion that the factory was 'very spooky, particularly at night, with strange lights, explosions and steam rising from various points'.[8] Whilst fulfilling an extremely important role in the war effort, there is little doubt that ROF 55 was a strange place - 'like something out of an H.G.Wells novel' I once heard someone comment. The factory bore little resemblance to a conventional one, consisting of some 2,000 or so small buildings. These were separated from each other by substantial distances and often large earth mounds and walls to reduce the risk of explosions. But for all this, the place had a wonderful working atmosphere and camaradarie. At its peak, Swynnerton employed between 20-30,000 personnel, the majority females aged between 18-35 years. Many lived locally in specially provided halls of residence and here they organised a remarkable social life for themselves including dances, film shows, pageants, and pantomimes. The Fledgling girls were invited to attend these events, which they did. However, when the American troops moved into nearby Nelson Hall, the social life was even further enhanced! Even so, many of the former Wrens carry memories of the ROF girls' yellow complexions and hair resulting from their work, and they were thankful not to be in a similar position.[9]

The Fledgling personnel contributed in no small way to the social scene themselves. There was a wealth of talent amongst their ranks - singers, dancers, instrumentalists, and this revealed itself in shows that were staged at the station or, on occasion, at venues in the district. Many of these performances were organised by CPO Tim Gavin, an instructor from HMS Daedalus II. Of all who served at the two establishments the name of Tim Gavin

Morning Divisions at HMS Fledgling, Mill Meece, July 1943.

Courtesy Mrs M Kennedy

Visit of King George and Queen Elizabeth to ROF Swynnerton, Feb. 1942.

stands out more than any other as one who set out to enrich the social life of service personnel in the area. This popular and highly respected officer is recalled with affection by those who recognise his great contribution to their entertainment during the dark days of the war. The girls also responded to the war effort on the home front by assisting with harvesting on nearby farms, their help much appreciated by the local community. But, in any event, the girls enjoyed the experience, pleased to be able to leave their studies and be out in the fresh air and sun, if only temporarily.[10]

According to local historian Norman Cope, over 1,500 Wrens had successfully completed their training at HMS Fledgling by Christmas 1944.[11] In October of that year, the first of a number of Canadian ground crew also arrived at Mill Meece for training as Air Mechanics. Approximately 420 eventually qualified and went on to form the nucleus of the Canadian Fleet Air Arm (later the Royal Canadian Naval Air Arm).[12] In addition, after the liberation of Holland, 240 Dutch ground crew qualified at the establishment. They eventually returned to their country to help rebuild the Marine Luchtvaar Dienst (Dutch Fleet Air Arm).[13]

HMS Fledgling closed in 1945 after hostilities ceased, although the Admiralty continued to use the premises for other purposes for a period.

NOTES

1. 'HMS Fledgling's Women Mechanics' in The Aeroplane 6th August 1943. pp154-158
2. Navy lists (various)
3. Frank Plant. Letter to author 20th April 1998
4. The Aeroplane op.cit
5. Ibid
6. Diary of Mrs A.D. Deacon. IWM 89/17/1
7. Mrs Amy Mansfield. Letter to author 23rd September 1998
8. Mrs Jean Williams. Letter to author 30th June 1997
9. M.H. Fletcher The WRNS (Batsford) p62
10. Mr J. Bennison Snr. Interview with author 3rd March 1997
11. Norman A. Cope. Stone in Staffordshire (Wood, Mitchell & Co, Hanley 1972) p142
12. The writer is most grateful to Ken West & Don Field (Canada) for information on this matter
13. The writer is also most appreciative of the assistance of Gerard Mutsaars (Holland) in helping to gather information on this aspect of Fledgling's history

September 1945: Thanksgiving Week in the centre of Newcastle-under-Lyme. Parading before the Mayor are Daedalus buglers (Left to Right) Bill Tomplinson (Kepple Division), Norman Mason, Ron Watt, Peter Smith (Effingham Division).

Courtesy Norman Mason

13th December 1945: Alderman & Mrs F T Brant, Mayor and Mayoress of Newcastle, bidding farewell to Captain (E) C A Shaw CBE, RN, at a special dinner given by the Mayor for officers and wives of HMS Daedalus, at the Castle Hotel.

Courtesy Evening Sentinel

Chapter Fourteen
VICTORY

In May 1945, the war against Germany came to an end. 'Victory in Europe Day', otherwise VE Day, saw a great explosion of excitement and celebration and is generally remembered by those who witnessed it. For some, however, the war was far from over. There remained the continued deadly conflict in the Far East, with millions of allied troops still engaged in fighting the Japanese.

Ignoring this, people organised street parties locally with borrowed trestle tables hastily erected in the carriageways. Despite rationing, a concerted effort was made to provide the best possible spread, with special treats for the children. Bunting was strung between properties, Union Jacks hung from bedroom windows and streets became a blaze of colour. The sound of laughter was heard from the children, none of them probably realising the importance of the occasion. In addition, pianos were moved outside to provide music for dancing. Victory bonfires were also arranged as part of the celebrations. One of the earliest of these took place on 7th May in Trentham Park. On the following day, the local 'Sentinel' newspaper heralded the event as 'a funeral pyre of Nazism' - a reference to logs for the blaze having been collected by German Prisoners of War.

At HMS Daedalus II a bonfire was built at the station's hangar site at Northwood Lane. It was ceremoniously lit by the 4 year old son of Lt (E) R.G.Swift, one of whose earliest memories is of the event and "being pushed to the front of the crowd' to ignite the huge pile of wood which had been hurriedly gathered.[1]

Official celebrations in Newcastle-under-Lyme included a Victory Parade and thanksgiving service. The Sentinel's report of the event describes the parade as one of the largest ever seen in the town, attended by huge crowds despite occasional rain. Special mention is made of the Royal Navy band and contingent being in attendance with the comment that they 'made a smart turn out'. After the parade all those participating joined the Mayor and Mayoress (Alderman & Mrs F.T. Brant) for the service of thanksgiving at St Giles Parish Church. The church was packed, according to the newspaper, and the service was relayed by tannoy to the crowds outside in Red Lion Square.[2]

Whilst some have vague memories of joining in the celebrations locally, others from Daedalus II celebrated elsewhere. Consequently, they are not aware of what happened in North Staffordshire. For example, Ron Watt (Effingham Division) spent VE Day in Liverpool at the home of a fellow apprentice. Having hitch-hiked to the city, they were 'royally entertained', before returning to Stoke by train in the early hours of the morning. Unfortunately, like a number of others, they arrived back at Clayton Hall '4 hours adrift' having only been granted leave until midnight. The following morning saw them on a long line of Commander's defaulters, all late arrivals, and offenders were lined up in the order in which they had reported to the guardroom. According to Ron, there were so many defaulters that, having walked some two-thirds of the line, the Commander dismissed those that he had already passed, and dished out punishment to the poor unfortunates remaining![3] Some former apprentices have recollections of visiting public houses in Newcastle and Stoke and then joining in the popular 'hokey cokey' and conga dances in the streets. Others have no doubt that the festivities and celebrations took place but, in fact, have no recollection of them. A few simply recall a feeling of disbelief that the war was over, followed by an immense sense of relief. They were not alone in this respect.

As 8th May dawned, there was a sense of elation generally that the war in Europe had come to an end, but the war against Japan was then to gain momentum. Thousands of tons of bombs were dropped on Tokyo by American bombers and in August atomic bombs were unleashed on Hiroshima and Nagasaki. As a result, on 15th August, Emperor Hirohito broadcast to his people that the war was over, and on 2nd September General MacArthur accepted the Japanese surrender on the USS Missouri in Tokyo Bay. Finally, on 12th September in Singapore, Admiral Mountbatten accepted the unconditional surrender of all Japanese forces in South East Asia.

VJ Day (Victory over Japan) on 15th August 1945 saw a further upsurge of joy and celebrations. Over at Mill Meece, the girls at HMS Fledgling carried the wardroom piano out onto the grass and sang songs while having a 'wonderful bonfire'. This was 'crowned by an effigy of Emperor Hirohito which was duly burned'. One former 2nd Officer Wren recalled 'splicing the main brace' to commemorate the occasion - her first taste of rum, but she 'didn't like it much!' In her diary, she commented that 'strictly speaking, WRNS personnel are not entitled to splice the main brace - but one doesn't win a war everyday. I only had half a tot, but had to disguise that with orange in order to drink it!' In the evening a variety show was held, followed by a dance, but as in the case of VE Day earlier, many couldn't comprehend that the war was over.[4]

World War II was the worst war of all, so far as casualties were concerned. The death toll figures vary, according to the reference books. However, the eminent historian Sir Martin Gilbert puts the figure at 50 million, and this includes soldiers of every nation involved in the conflict, together with civilian casualties.[5] Even so, official figures will never tell the true story of bravery, pain and loss, or the devastating effect on families and relationships. There were also those who, having lost loved ones, or had them seriously wounded, were left wondering whether the cost was really worth the price.

NOTES

1. Graham W. Swift. Interview with author 14th September 1998
2. Sentinel 14th May 1945
3. Ron Watt op.cit
4. Mrs A.D. Deacon op.cit
5. Sir Martin Gilbert The Day The War Ended (Harper Collins) p101

Chapter Fifteen
DEPARTURE

The coming of peace inevitably led to the departure of HMS Daedalus II from North Staffordshire. News of the Admiralty's decision to relocate the training establishment was first reported to Newcastle Borough Council on 4th October 1945[1], with a subsequent announcement in the local press later that month.[2]

As preparations to move the 1,300 personnel to HMS Condor, Arbroath, got underway, a number of functions were arranged to bid farewell to the crew. Amongst these was a dinner at the town's Castle Hotel at which Captain (E) C.A. Shaw CBE, RN, Officer Commanding, presented a plaque, featuring the figure of Daedalus, to the Mayor, Alderman F.T. Brant. In expressing appreciation for the gift, the Mayor wished the crew 'all happiness in their new home', adding that 'the town had been pleased to receive the officers and men of the RNATE and would be sorry to see the establishment go.' The Deputy Mayor, Alderman J.H. Ramsbotham spoke in similar vein thanking the officers and men 'for the great help' that they had given to the Mayoralty in connection with various appeals for the war effort, in particular National Savings. Other members of the Council echoed the sentiments including Alderman J. Kelly JP, who said that since coming to Newcastle, the establishment had been 'a great credit to the town.' In response, Captain Shaw said that 'all the people of Newcastle had been very good to the establishment' and he regarded it 'as luck that Admiral Ford should have a brother here as Mayor of the town' when it became necessary to evacuate from Lympne.[3]

Not to be outdone, the apprentices held their own farewell dance at the Municipal Hall on 7th December. The hall was reported as being appropriately festooned with the flags of the Allies and more than 600 danced the night away to the music provided by the RNATE band led by Eddie Jackson. Naval apprentice P.G. Teale acted as MC for the evening while refreshments were provided free of charge by the YMCA voluntary workers. In appreciation of the hospitality and kindness shown to the members of all the services during the war period, the YMCA Canteen Organiser, Mrs E.W. Good, was formally presented with a wireless set for the local Branch. Speaking on behalf of the Canteen Committee, Mrs Ford expressed regret that the establishment was leaving Newcastle, and said that 'it had been a pleasure to do what they could to help the apprentices'. Finally, the Mayor, in his farewell speech, said that he hoped that the apprentices 'would take away with them many happy memories'.[4]

Later, the Council instructed the Town Clerk, Mr J. Griffith, to write to the Admiralty expressing 'deep regret' at the leaving of the RNATE. He wrote of his belief that 'the relationship between the establishment and the town had always been of a most satisfactory nature, and will long be remembered with pleasure. The conduct of the ratings has been exemplary' he continued, 'and the establishment has in many ways been a valuable asset. They have set an example in good behaviour and bearing to the townspeople generally and other troops in the area'.[5]

In response, the Secretary to the Lords of the Admiralty wrote that 'cordial relations which have always existed between the Naval Establishment and the Borough have always been a source of much gratification'. In addition, 'the attitude of all owners of requisitioned buildings and grounds has always been most helpful and co-operative'.[6]

In the meantime, those members of the ship's company and trainees remaining at the establishment were busily engaged in dismantling equipment and packaging it for transportation. Don Drayton (Raleigh Division) and Alf Richardson (Effingham Division) can well recall being employed in this capacity.[7] All training divisions left Newcastle-under-Lyme in December 1945. Raleigh, Effingham & Keppel Divisions proceeded to HMS Condor, Arbroath, whilst Hood was diverted to HMS Kestrel at Worthy Down. Sick Berth Attendant Fred Lovell also had the thankless task of packing up all the medical equipment for transportation. Having been one of the first arrivals at Newcastle, Fred claims to be the last of the ship's company to leave. He was discharged in the town from naval service on 22nd January 1946.[8]

The Admiralty went on to release requisitioned property gradually during that year. As far as the Council was concerned, the earliest to be released were the Municipal Hostel and Old Bank House in February.[9]

The Westlands Girls' School followed, a month later[10], but, strange as it may appear, parts of the Clayton Hall Estate were still in the hands of the Admiralty in March 1947.[11] In the meantime, the Council had been notified that the Admiralty intended to retain the hangars and workshops in Northwood Lane permanently.[12]

NOTES

1. NBC. Minutes of General Purposes (Education) Sub-Committee
2. Sentinel 30th October 1945
3. Sentinel 14th December 1945
4. Sentinel 8th December 1945
5. NBC. Minutes of General Purposes Committee 28th January 1946
6. NBC. -ditto- 25th February 1946
7. Interviews with author 18th September 1996
8. Certificate of discharge (copy in author's collection)
9. NBC. Minutes of Housing (Management) Sub-Committee 4th February 1946 and Postwar Planning & Reconstruction Sub-Committee 15th February 1946
10. NBC. Minutes of Education Committee 18th March 1946
11. NBC. Minutes of General Purposes Committee 25th March 1947
12. NBC. Minutes of Education Committee 20th May 1946
    Note: These premises became an RN Transport Depot. It closed in 1959 (see Victoria County History Vol 8 p76)

1944. 2nd Grenville Division apprentices, with officers and instructors, in front of the camouflaged Clayton Hall.

Courtesy J Williams

June 1944. 2nd Benbow Division apprentices on passing out, with Divisional Commander Lt Hendy, Lt Commander Carlisle and Commander Rothwell (centre).

Courtesy J Fowler

Clayton Hall 1945. Rear Admiral Trowbridge inspects Hood Division during his annual tour of HMS Daedalus.

Courtesy Newcastle Borough Museum

Chapter Sixteen
IN RETROSPECT

Information supplied to the media in late 1945 indicates that 4,245 personnel were successfully trained at HMS Daedalus II during the RNATE's period at Newcastle-under-Lyme. This figure consists of Air Apprentices (1,513); Air Fitters (2,101); Air Mechanics (600); and WRNS Air Mechanics (31). All went on to serve in ships and stations in the various theatres of war.[1]

The success rate of the establishment was, no doubt, aided by the relationship with the Council and the Borough in general. Indeed, comments of the Admiralty in a letter to the Council confirm their mutual good feelings. Writing to the Town Clerk, the correspondent speaks of the 'cordial relations which have always existed between the Naval Establishment and the Borough' saying that these had 'contributed very materially to the efficient training which has been received'.[2] A contemporary report for the Ministry of Information speaks similarly of 'Newcastle being a happy choice regarding relocation, for it is an agreeable Staffordshire market town'. The report also comments that despite the dispersal of training buildings, the system 'seemed a triumph of ingenious administration over difficulties'.[3]

The actor/screenwriter John Hale, himself a former apprentice of 2nd Benbow Division, whilst commenting that his early training was 'not much fun', nevertheless acknowledges that 'Clayton Hall was a decently run place' and that 'the local people were good to us'.[4] John White (also formerly of 2nd Benbow Division) writes of the 'exceptional allegiance' and 'esprit de corps' which existed amongst the training divisions and which, no doubt, aided the success of Daedalus II.[5] Another former apprentice wrote that it is a tribute to Newcastle-under-Lyme and the training received that 'the transfer of maintenance responsibilities from the RAF to the Fleet Air Arm went so well and led in no small measure to the FAA becoming the major force in the Royal Navy'. In addition, he contends that 'almost all' of the Technical Instructors in the FAA from the 1950s to the late 1970s, and the Chief Artificers, who governed naval aircraft maintenance in all our ships and stations during that period, were initially trained at Daedalus II.[6]

Not surprisingly, a number of personnel from Daedalus married local girls and have remained in the North Staffordshire area. Others moved with their new partners to other parts of the country or abroad. However, they continue to hold regular reunions, some of which are in the North Staffordshire area, and numbers return to old haunts to refresh their memories of the war years. Clayton Hall is naturally high on the list of venues revisited, and in 1994 former members of the 2nd Benbow Division held a special service of thanksgiving and remembrance at the premises. To this day, that same esprit de corps remains amongst all the former Daedalus II personnel that I have had the privilege of meeting. In my view, they remain a remarkable group of men and women, each of whom contributed in a small, but significant way during a critical period in British, and indeed, world history.

As for Clayton Hall, little evidence now remains of the Daedalus II era, other than the gymnasium and the chapel, now used as a store. At the time of writing, the concrete bases of the former 'P' huts are in the process of being removed. After the war the Hall eventually became the home of Clayton Hall Grammar School for Girls, but today is that of Clayton High School. The hangar site in Northwood Lane subsequently became a RN Transport Depot. After its closure in 1959, the site was eventually redeveloped with housing.

NOTES

1. Sentinel 30th October 1945
2. NBC. Admiralty to Town Clerk 23rd February 1946
3. Report of Major Owen Rutter. IWM 85/10/5
4. John Hale. Letter to author 15th March 1997
5. John White. Letter to author 25th April 1996
6. The correspondent, a retired Lt. Cdr, wishes to remain anonymous (correspondence in author's private collection).

11th July 1990: Presentation of Daedalus Plaques to Newcastle Mayor Councillor J Whalley by (Left to Right) Cyril Girling, Jack Carnill and a petty officer from HMS Daedalus, Lee on Solent.

Courtesy Evening Sentinel

S.1559 (Established June 1943)

CERTIFICATE OF DISCHARGE (INTERIM) FROM NAVAL SERVICE

(Available for six months only from the date of issue)

This Interim Certificate of Discharge, which is evidence that the rating has been finally discharged from the Naval Service, takes the place of the Service Certificate until that is received. It is a valid discharge for the purposes of claims to Health and Unemployment Benefits.

This is to Certify that Frederick Thomas LOYELL

Official No. R.N.B.S. B.R. [illegible]

lately serving as Sick Berth Attendant entered the Royal Navy ~~Women's Royal Naval Service~~

on 4th September 1939 is on leave ~~pending~~ discharge ~~has been discharged therefrom~~

and is free to take up civil employment forthwith.

General character Very Good Date of Birth 9 June 1921

Height 5 ft. 7 ins. Colour of Hair Brown

Date of final discharge 20 March 1946 Colour of Eyes Grey

SHIP'S STAMP
R.N. ARTIFICER
Training Establishment
21 JAN [illegible]
CAPTAIN'S OFFICE
NEWCASTLE, STAFFS.

[signature]
CAPTAIN (E) RN.
COMMANDING OFFICER

Date 22nd January 1946

TO BE RETURNED AT ONCE ON RECEIPT OF SERVICE CERTIFICATE.

Municipal Hall, Newcastle, 7 December 1945: Farewell dance for members of HMS Daedalus. Front Row L to R: Mr R Eady, Mrs R M Ford, Mayor & Mayoress F T Brant, Capt (E) C A Shaw CBE, RN, Mrs W M Truswell, Mrs E W Good.

Courtesy Evening Sentinel

BENBOW DIVISION AIR APPRENTICES

1941 - 1944

AN ACT OF THANKSGIVING
AND REMEMBRANCE

H.M.S. DAEDALUS II

CLAYTON HALL, NEWCASTLE UNDER LYME

*Clayton Hall, photographed by the author in 1996.
Now the home of Clayton High School.*

*Remains of 'P' Hut accommodation, with Clayton Hall in the background.
Photographed by the author in 1996.*

All that remains of the 'P' Hut accommodation of HMS Daedalus II. Photographed by the author in 1996.

Newcastle Mayor, Councillor Mrs E Caddy, takes the salute during the march past of the 2nd Benbow Division Veterans. Clayton Hall, 26th June 1994.

Courtesy J Carnill

26th June 1994: Newcastle Mayor, Councillor Mrs E Caddy JP, inspects former members of the 2nd Benbow Division at Clayton Hall (now Clayton High School) on the occasion of their reunion. The Mayor is escorted by her husband as consort, former Chief Petty Officer apprentice 'Sam' Selman (in peaked cap).

Courtesy Evening Sentinel

Appendix

Commanding Officers of HMS Daedalus II

Captain (E) B.L.G. Sebastian	1939 - 1941
Captain (E) J.I. Moore	1941 - 1944
Captain (E) C.A. Shaw CBE	1944 - 1945

Apprentice Training Divisions at Clayton Hall

1st Benbow	June 1940 - June 1942
1st Rodney	December 1940 - December 1942
1st Grenville	December 1940 - December 1942
1st Anson	September 1940 - June 1943
2nd Rodney	January 1942 - December 1943
2nd Benbow	September 1942 - June 1944
2nd Grenville	January 1943 - December 1944
2nd Anson	September 1943 - June 1945
Hood	January 1944 - December 1945
Raleigh	June 1944 - December 1945
Effingham	January 1945 - December 1945
Keppel	June 1945 - December 1945

Bibliography

In addition to those works quoted in the source notes, I found the following particularly useful:

RAF Squadrons	Wing Commander E.G. Jefford	Airlife Publishing Ltd
The Squadrons of the Fleet Air Arm	R. Sturtivant & T. Ballance	Air-Britain
RAF at War	Ed. Sir C. Foxley-Norris	Ian Allan Ltd
A Positive Page	A. Ryles	Private publication
The Story of the WRNS	Eileen Bigland	Nicholson & Watson
The WRNS	M.H. Fletcher	Batsford
Blue for a Girl	John D. Drummond	W.H. Allen
Tienduizend Vrije Vogels	R.E. van Holst	Pellekaan De Batafsche Leeuw
Certified Serviceable	Ed.P. Charlton & M. Whitby	Publishing Plus (Ottawa)

Abbreviations

In the text and source notes, abbreviations denote the following:

PRO	Public Record Office
IWM	Imperial War Museum
NBC	Newcastle Borough Council
FAA	Fleet Air Arm
RNATE	Royal Navy Artificer Training Establishment
PO	Petty Officer
CPO	Chief Petty Officer
NCO	Non-Commissioned Officer
RPO	Regimental Police Officer